HANDY HINTS FOR GARDENERS

Over 300 A - Z tips

KEITH KIRSTEN

NEW HOLLAND

ACKNOWLEDGEMENTS

I would like to acknowledge all those great gardeners out there, both amateur and professional, who have never ceased to inspire and enlighten me with their gardening pursuits. I'm sure many of the tips in this book will be familiar to you, but I hope that at least some of them will be new.

My sincerest thanks and appreciation to Edgar Rosenberg, horticulturist and man of many talents, for assisting in the compilation of this book.

To Lizelle Meyer-Faedda, Helen Bloom and Shirley Wallington for their assistance, and Mynderd Vosloo for his fun illustrations.

Last, but most definitely not least, to the team from Struik Publishers for their continuous enthusiasm and input, in particular Annlerie van Rooyen, Dominique le Roux, Lesley Hay-Whitton and Alison Day.

FOREWORD

In today's world where one never seems to have enough time to complete life's tasks, be they work or play, we are constantly looking for quick and easy tips to achieve results. Gardening, considered internationally as the most popular pastime, is no exception. Hopefully these helpful tips will be awesome for the beginner gardener, yet also challenging for the most experienced. I trust they will go a long way to making gardening even more pleasurable and rewarding. And don't forget: when it comes to weeds, one year's seeding makes seven years' weeding!

ANNUALS

GROW ANNUALS FROM SEED TO SAVE MONEY

Instead of buying trays of seedlings, buy the seeds and grow them yourself – either sow these in specially prepared seed trays or buy ready-mixed seed-packs in the colour of your choice and simply sprinkle them in the areas of your garden where you would like more colour. Seeds such as violas, primulas, Virginia stocks and nasturtiums can easily be scattered in situ. Seeds are economical to buy and from a single packet of seed one can obtain many plants, especially if you are planting large areas under colour. The instructions on the back of the seed pack will tell you exactly how they must be handled to achieve success.

Also see Seed Sowing tips

KEEP SEEDLINGS WELL WATERED

To ensure that they have had a good drink of water and won't wilt, water plants in their trays at least an hour before planting them out. Always plant out all the seedlings when you get them home, as the trays hold very little soil and are prone to drying out very quickly.

If by some accident the tray has dried out and the plants are showing signs of wilting, immerse the entire tray, plants and all, in a bath of water. Leave them there for at least 20 minutes and they should perk up again. Weigh down polystyrene trays with a brick or heavy object as it is important that the entire plant is under water if you want to save it – bear in mind that plants can absorb water through their leaves.

Water seedlings well after planting and keep them moist until they have established themselves. This will take at least two weeks.

Also see Watering tips

SELECT TOUGH SEEDLING TYPES

Choose annuals that do not need much care other than a regular watering – look out for those with a long flowering season, rain- and drought-tolerance, and those that don't need deadheading. Good examples include marigolds, lobelia, petunias, impatiens, violas and pansies.

PICK MORE FOR MORE FLOWERS

The good news for lovers of cut flowers is the fact that the more you pick them, the more the likes of poppies, sweetpeas, primulas, pansies and violas will produce.

Also see Cut Flowers tips

CHOOSE YOUR SEEDLINGS CAREFULLY

● Look for trays of plants that are not rootbound or fully in flower – at this young stage the plants should be putting all their energy into growing rather than producing flowers. To check whether they are rootbound, gently remove one or two plants from their tray and look at the roots, which should not be growing in a tight hard ball or circle. If they are, you will have to tease the roots apart and loosen them slightly when planting so that they all face outwards around the entire root ball of the plant. Also ensure they all have a bright white growing tip. If the seedlings have been rootbound and in the trays too long they might be slightly stunted and will take additional time to grow out. Given the correct conditions, they should do so reasonably quickly.

● Choose the trays that have smaller, healthy plants of good green colour with no pale or yellowing leaves. Look out for signs of disease. For example, wilting leaves and drooping or shrivelled stems might be the first sign of a disease called 'damping off', which is a common soil-borne disease in seedlings. If you find that, once planted, the little seedlings start dying for no apparent reason, despite your having given them ideal growing conditions as required by the instructions on their label, then treat the soil with a product to prevent damping off. Overwatering and warm soil conditions help the disease to spread to other seedlings.

USE COLOUR TO ATTRACT ATTENTION

Annuals are great for creating splashes of colour in high profile areas such as the front entrance to your house, on the patio or around a formal pond. Save money by concentrating the colour in a small area or where it is easily seen and creates the most effect. Colourful annuals are also excellent as fillers between plants or as focal points to highlight features such as a large pot, a garden seat or sculpture.

Also see Colour tips

REMOVE SEEDLINGS GENTLY

Never pull seedlings out by the stem as they are likely to break off at soil level. Instead, remove annuals from soft plastic or polystyrene trays by pushing up with your fingers from underneath so that the entire soil ball comes out. Do not apply too much pressure on any part of the plant when holding or removing it, as you can cause bruising or damage. However, if there are small white roots emerging from the bottom of the tray, there is no need to worry about breaking these as they will grow again.

ALLOW YOUNG ROOTS TWICE THE SPACE

When planting seedlings into the soil, be sure to dig the holes big enough – you don't want to force the young new roots into a hole that is smaller than the root ball, as this may bruise them. Dig a hole at least twice the size of the root ball that you have removed from the tray. Place the plant in the hole, gently fill in the soil and press down firmly.

SPACE FOR THE FUTURE, NOT THE PRESENT

When planting annuals in beds, plant them at their recommended spacing. Annuals are fast growers and will cover the allotted space in no time at all. You will also save money by sticking to the planting width recommended on the label. When planting rows of seedlings, always space them alternately as you plant them (from the back to the front) so that as they grow they will fill the spaces left around them. This will also prevent you from getting a straight row effect as viewed from the front when they do flower.

1st ROW

2nd ROW

3rd ROW

SAVE WATER BY CREATING A BOG GARDEN

If you want to plant beautiful subjects such as gunnera, rodgersia, and moisture-loving primulas which require lots of water or swampy conditions, simply create a bog garden. Dig a hole of appropriate size and depth, line it with heavy-duty plastic bags, opened and trimmed to size if necessary, and add enough water to form a pool at the bottom. Then add your compost and soil mixture, plant your moisture-lovers in the bog garden and water well. Thereafter water normally – the water at the bottom acts as a reservoir and the plastic liner prevents the water from being dissipated into the adjacent soil.

GET PERFECT FORM WITH AN OUTLINE

Lay a hosepipe in full sun to soften, then drag it to form pleasant shapes and smooth curves along the edges of your beds. Now simply cut out the shape of the bed using the hosepipe as your outline.

START BEDS WITH A RIGHT ANGLE

When starting a bed from a wall, paving or any solid thing in your garden, bring the flower bed out at a 90° angle from that position before you start the curve. Never try to run a bed right up to a wall or steps at an acute angle as you end up with a long, narrow strip of bed that is difficult to plant in and whose edge is difficult to keep straight when cutting the edges of the lawn.

MAKE MAINTENANCE EASIER

To avoid continually having to trim growth back, make paths wider than you want the end product to be, so that plants have room to spread out and soften the edges without obstructing the walkway.

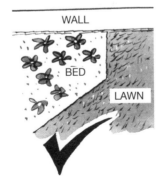

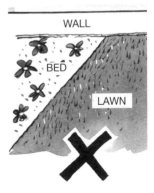

BULBS

KEEP BULBS COOL

Do not leave bulbs lying around in the sun before planting as the heat could damage the embryonic leaf and flower buds, which have developed within the bulbs and are just waiting to shoot up after they have been planted.

CHOOSE LONG-LIVED BULBS

Consider using bulbs that are long lived, as opposed to those that will only give you a one-off display. For example, daffodils and narcissi, scillas, cyclamen, muscari and crocuses will give you much pleasure over many years without your having to lift and replant them every season. These bulbs will also multiply in the garden. After a few years you can lift the bulbs when they are dormant, separate them and plant the extras elsewhere – you should soon have enough to start giving away to friends.

DISGUISE DYING SPRING FOLIAGE

Interplant summer-flowering daylilies (*Hemerocallis*) with spring-flowering bulbs like daffodils, tulips and hyacinths, as they will disguise the ugly, dying leaves of the bulbs with their fresh new foliage. By early summer this bulb foliage will have vanished beneath the leaves of the daylilies with which they are interplanted and the daylilies will have started to flower, very soon providing a mass of colour.

WATER CAREFULLY

The area in which the bulbs have been planted should be watered thoroughly after planting and mulched with a blanket of garden compost. Do not water again until the soil below the mulch is dry. Overwatering can be fatal. More anemones and tulips, for instance, fail through too much water being applied than for any other reason.
Also see Watering tips

USE SHARP SAND TO PREVENT ROTTING

The bulbs of lilies, tuberous begonias, amaryllis, dahlias and others that are susceptible to rotting should be surrounded with a few handfuls of clean, sharp sand to improve the drainage around the bulb.

BUY QUALITY BULBS

When buying bulbs, tubers, corms or rhizomes, select the largest, fattest and heaviest that you can find. This will make sure that they are full of energy for new growth.

LAYER BULBS FOR EXTENDED FLOWERING

Plant different types of bulbs in the same container at different levels. Start with the bulbs that need the deepest soil at the bottom, then add the next layer of bulbs and then the most shallow-growing ones in the uppermost layer. (Look for planting instructions on the packet that the bulbs are sold in.) This way your pot of bulbs will flower over an extended period rather than just one lot of the same bulbs that all flower at the same time. You can also plant the same type of bulb in a container at different heights. The bulbs that are planted the deepest will take the longest to emerge and flower. Plant some annuals or low-growing plants in the top of the soil to act as a groundcover. White alyssum and parsley make wonderful companion plants for bulbs planted in pots and act as a foil for their flowers.

SOAK BULBS BEFORE PLANTING

Hard, dry bulbs such as ranunculus and anemones can do with an overnight soaking before planting to give them a head start. In fact the instructions on their packets will often suggest this, but this advice also applies to begonias, dahlias, amaryllis and iris which should have fat juicy stems. If you see any of these bulbs showing signs of shrivelling, soak them in a bucket of water for a few hours before planting.

PROTECT AGAINST MOLES

Avoid the heartache of damage caused by moles eating your newly planted bulbs by lining the holes with a wire basket or specialized plastic planting cage custom-made for this purpose. You can also line the hole with wire mesh or special planting bags made with perishable fabric. Dig the hole for the bulbs slightly bigger than you would usually require and line it with the wire. Place some soil on the base of the cage and plant bulbs as recommended. The wire will eventually rust away if you do not remember to lift it after the bulbs have flowered.

Also see Pests & Diseases tips

WIRE MESH

REMEMBER WHERE YOU PLANTED

Mark all bulbs that die down after flowering to avoid damaging them by digging there later. Use any material that will not fade or disintegrate. This way they will also be much easier to find if you need to move them once the leaves have disappeared.

DON'T LEAVE AIR POCKETS

It is important to make sure that the bottom of the bulb makes firm contact with the soil beneath it, before you cover the top with soil.

GET THE DEPTH RIGHT

The general rule to be followed here is that the bulb must be planted and covered by soil at a depth of twice the *height* of the bulb. In other words, if your bulb is 5cm (2in) tall it needs to be covered by 10cm (4in) of soil. However, if planted deeper than the recommended depth, most bulbs will survive but just take longer to flower.

KNOW YOUR UPS AND DOWNS

It is sometimes difficult to tell which is the top of some bulbs — the ranunculus and anemone are particularly common culprits. Once you have soaked these two species overnight in a bucket of water, drain the water off, and plant as follows:

● The 'claws' of the ranunculus must face downwards. You will see a small, flat piece of the bulb where all the claws meet once you turn the bulb the right way up. This is the top. When planting ranunculus that have been soaked, remember that they are quite brittle, so be careful not to apply too much pressure to the claws when inserting them into the soil, as they may break off. The claws are the storage roots needed for the bulb to grow and must therefore be kept on the plant at all costs.

● Anemone corms should be planted point downwards. It is not always easy to decide which side has the point so, if in doubt, let the plant do the thinking. Plant the corm on its side and, as the foliage develops, it will be swung automatically into the correct position.

● Most other bulbs will have an onion shape, with a broad flat bottom and a narrow neck, and so will be easy to plant correctly: the narrow, thin part at the top and the broader, fatter part of the bulb resting on the soil.

CLIMBERS & CREEPERS

KEEP PLANTS OFF THE WALL

Creeper-covered trellises attached to walls or fences make painting difficult, if not impossible. Instead, hang the trellis panels on a wall or fence with large, sturdy hooks – depending on the size of the panels, six hooks should suffice, with two at the top, middle and bottom of each panel. When painting time comes around, simply lift the trellis, with plants attached, off the hooks and gently lay it down so that you can get to the surface to be painted.

BE EXTRAVAGANT

When trying to cover large areas of wall or fence, plant climbers far closer than the recommended distances. Creepers do not mind being too cramped, as they will just find their own sunlight. In this way you will cover the entire area far more quickly. Plant climbers well away (at least 40cm/16in) from the base of any wall to keep it away from the concrete foundation – place a stake at an angle to the wall and train the first stems along this.

MATCHING PLANTS TO ASPECT

It is vital to choose climbers to match the conditions on offer. The direction a wall or fence faces (north, south, east or west) makes a huge difference to what plants will do well there as it will affect whether the surface is in sun or shade. Many climbers will do well in a sunny situation on a south-facing wall, including passionflower (*Passiflora*), Potato vine (*Solanum*), campsis, actinidia, roses and wisteria. North-facing walls are in deep shade all day and far fewer plants will thrive there. Choose ivies, honeysuckles or Russian vine (*Fallopia*). Other climbers will tolerate some shade, including many clematis, hops (*Humulus lupulus*), ornamental grape vines (*Vitis*), parthenocissus and the climbing hydrangea (*Hydrangea anomala petiolaris*).

COASTAL GARDENING

RINSE THOSE LEAVES

If you live near the coast and your garden receives salt-laden spray from the sea, rinse off the salt deposits on leaves before the sun gets to them in the mornings. This will prevent the salt drawing moisture out of the leaf and will also prevent salt burn on the leaves.

USE A WINDBREAK

Plant a windbreak of tall-growing plants against the prevailing wind. In this way, most of the salt gets deposited on this decoy and so less finds its way onto your beds on the leeward side.

LEACH THE SALT OUT

To prevent salt deposits building up in your soil, be sure to water the garden beds thoroughly, in so doing leaching out the salt and taking it lower down into the soil past the roots of your plants. Face the fact, however, that this will be an ongoing battle with the elements.

COLOUR

DECEIVE THE EYE

To make a small garden appear larger than it is, plant pale, soft colours farthest away from the house or the main viewing area of the garden, for example the patio or front door, and use hot, vivid colours in the foreground.

To make a narrow garden look broader than it is, plant bright flowering plants towards the back and grow paler, softer colours towards the middle of the garden.
Also see Container Types tips

REMEMBER THAT GREEN IS ALSO A COLOUR

Different shades of green can be used very effectively in a garden's overall design for contrast and texture. Broadly speaking, always choose a shrub or tree, or any plant for that matter, on its leaf texture and the shape of the plant. If it happens to give you flowers, think of these as a bonus. Flowering trees and shrubs only flower for short periods of time. For most of the year, you have to live with and look at the leaf texture and colour and the shape of the plant in the garden. So choose your plants well. Obviously there are exceptions – roses and annuals, for example, are grown specifically for their flowering capabilities.

LOOK AT THE LIGHT

The low angle of the sun at the start and end of the day highlights certain colours dramatically, so place plants in the garden where their colours will be best highlighted by the changes in the intensity of light. Early morning light has a reddish cast that accentuates warm-hued flowers and foliage. During late afternoon, lavenders, blues, creams and whites appear to glow in the light of dusk.

CONTAINER GARDENING

TAKE YOUR FAVOURITES WITH YOU

If you intend moving soon you can always lift some of your favourite plants, place them in containers or plastic bags and simply pack them up and take them with you to your new garden. If you happen to have enough empty pots, then use them for this purpose. However, the most economical option is the black plastic planting bags you can buy from your local nursery. Inexpensive and durable, they already have drainage holes and are available in pretty much any size you will need. Plants are usually quite happy in these bags for a fairly lengthy period, until you are ready to plant them in their new situation. In this way, provided you have enough plants from the previous garden, you can almost create an instant effect in the new one.

USE ROLLERS TO MOVE HEAVY POTS

To move very heavy pots and containers, use a system of round metal pipes to roll the pot along – if you can find perfectly round, hard, wooden ones such as old broom handles, these will also do. As the pipe at the back emerges, place it in front of the pot and in this way you can roll the pot along. Make sure that the pipes you are using are strong enough to take the weight of the container, that the pot has a flat base, and the terrain is hard and even.

LIFT TO CREATE MORE HEIGHT

If you are grouping containers together to create an effect and you find your collection lacks a bit of height, simply turn an empty pot upside down and use this as a pedestal for another container with a plant in it.

EMPTY CONTAINER UPSIDE DOWN

THE CONTAINER TO SUIT YOUR HEIGHT

Growing plants in pots or raised containers makes them easily accessible to those in wheelchairs or who are otherwise disabled. In this way, anybody can take part in gardening activities.

COVER THOSE EYESORES

Pots can cover a multitude of sins. Drains, manholes and other eyesores can be hidden by covering them with a container or a collection of pots which can easily be moved should you need to reach the very problem you're now trying to hide. Place a container on the top of a drain, for example, but remember however that you will almost certainly need to move it at some stage. So keep the pot size sensible, remembering that once it has a plant in it and you have added the water, it will be far heavier.

PUT LIKE WITH LIKE

When planting a variety of plants in the same pot, be sure to choose those that need the same growing conditions. It is pointless combining a shade-loving plant with sun-lovers in a sunny spot. The shade plant will not survive.
Also see Bulbs tips

DON'T PUT A SMALL PLANT IN A LARGE POT

When moving a plant into a new pot, use a pot that is only about twice the size of the one that the plant is growing in presently. If you make the new one too big, the soil in the pot can become sour and lifeless as there may not be enough roots to keep the soil alive. It can also lead to too much water retention, causing the soil to become waterlogged and devoid of the oxygen the plant roots need for the metabolism of nutrients.

JUST ADD BALLAST

When planting a very tall plant in a large pot, be aware of how easily the two could be blown over. To counteract this top-heaviness, add some ballast to the bottom of the pot: large, heavy stones will weigh it down, as will a heavy piece of steel or lead. Be sure, however, that you do not use up too much compost space.

LIGHTEN WINDOW BOXES

Instead of filling a window box directly with compost and plants, fill it with individual plastic flower pots, each with its own plant. Do, however, be prepared to water often. The handy thing is the simplicity with which you can replace one plant that has gone over with a new one, ensuring that your window box looks fantastic all year round.

ENSURE GOOD DRAINAGE

If you want to turn a container that does not have any holes into a plant pot, always remember to drill holes in it for drainage. Any form of container will then be suitable for cultivating plants. If, however, the pot is very valuable, you can still grow plants in it without drilling holes but be sure to watch the watering carefully. Plant in a slightly smaller, well-drained container and insert this into your cherished one. Containers without holes should not be used outside where they will get rained on. The container will be filled with water which will not be able to escape unless you go out after every rainfall or watering and tilt the pot on its side to drain it.

PLACE POTS ON FEET

Outdoor pots and containers can be placed on 'feet' of half bricks, special pot feet purchased from your local nursery, or any hard object to avoid poor drainage. The gap between the pot and the ground ensures better drainage of water, prevents the possibility of the formation of a water pocket, and counters the invasion of ants that might want to set up home in the container.

Another bonus is that the dryness of the air 'prunes' any of the roots that are trying to grow through the drainage holes of the pot. If any roots do manage to grow through the bottom of the pot, be sure to cut these off as you don't want them acting as a plug, especially if your pot only has a single drainage hole. If this does happen, use a knife or even a drill to cut away at the offending root and so ensure free drainage again. Whenever possible, lift or turn containers on their sides to check that roots are not growing through and blocking the escape route for the water, which might then drown the plant.

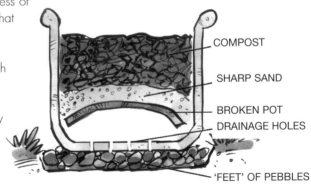

COMPOST

SHARP SAND

BROKEN POT
DRAINAGE HOLES

'FEET' OF PEBBLES

TRAP THE COMPOST, NOT THE WATER

Before filling a pot with compost, always use a dish-shaped piece of broken pot, called a crock, or any concave piece of material like a stone, and place it concave side down over each hole in the base of the pot. Then pour a layer of sharp sand (available at any good nursery) over this crock, followed by the compost. This will allow free drainage of water, but will trap the compost particles and prevent them filtering through and out of the pot, leaving their tell-tale discolouration marks on tiles or paving.

Another advantage of using sand in the bottom of the pot is that it prevents the roots from sticking to the pot when you're trying to remove the plant. The sand always remains loose and friable, keeping the roots loose as well. Always keep pieces of broken pot in a storeroom rather than throwing them away, just in case you need to use them later as crocks.

NEVER MIX YOUR FORMULAS

Only use special composts for the specific plants they were intended for. For example, use ericaceous compost for acid-loving plants, such as azaleas, camellias and hydrangeas, and bonsai compost only for bonsai. These composts are scientifically formulated to suit the requirements of the specified plant types. Wait until spring to replant those plants that seem not to be growing happily.

Also see Feeding tips

KEEP THE COMPOST SWEET

By adding charcoal to the potting mixture before planting, you can prevent the compost from souring in the pot. Use small chips of ordinary charcoal that you would normally use on the barbecue – three double handfuls of charcoal per large bag of compost should do it.

SOLVE BAD SOIL PROBLEMS

Containers are excellent for those plants that are not suited to your garden conditions. For example, if you are determined to have pink hydrangeas but the soil in your garden is on the acid side so perfect for blue hydrangeas, then simply plant the pink ones in containers with the appropriate soil. (Use a compost mixture that has had lime added to it, buy a specially formulated alkaline compost, or feed with hydrangea pink concentrate from nurseries.) Obviously, the reverse will apply if you are trying to grow blue hydrangeas in an alkaline soil.

SAVE ON COMPOST

When using deep containers that will use more compost than the plant or plants require, place chunks of polystyrene into the bottoms of the containers. Make sure you still retain a decent amount of compost. This will save on potting compost and provide excellent drainage.

CONTAIN THE COMPETITION

Containers can also be completely sunk into the ground to create a place to grow plants, especially useful in areas where there is too much competition from the roots of surrounding trees. Simply dig a hole the same size as the pot, which should be inserted deep enough to keep the rim level with the surrounding soil. Be sure to lift the pot out of the hole at least once or twice a year to check that the roots have not grown out of it. Never forget to give extra water to the plants in pots to prevent them drying out.

CONTAINER PLANTS – FEEDING & WATERING

WATERPROOF SAUCERS INSIDE THE HOME

When using saucers for indoor plants make sure that they are made either of glazed ceramic or plastic. A saucer made of a porous material such as terracotta will leave a horrible mark on wooden floors or furniture. The terracotta absorbs the water and then sweats it out, leaving unsightly white marks on furniture. Silicone waterproofing agents for painting the insides of saucers is available, but there is no guarantee this will prevent stains.

If a watermark does appear on any piece of furniture, wipe the area thoroughly with a clean, dry cloth and leave it for a few hours to dry out. Warm up a little petroleum jelly and pour it over the affected area, leave for at least 30 minutes, then give it a good hard rub with a soft, dry cloth.

PREVENT MUD SPLASHES

To prevent rapid water loss as well as compost splashing onto paving, walls or the plant's leaves as you water, place a layer of sharp sand, gravel, stones or wood chips as a mulch on top of the compost in the container.
Also see Mulching tips

AVOID THE BURN

Water plants a few hours before applying fertilizer, as dry roots will absorb the fertilizer mixture too quickly, causing the soft growing tips of the roots to be burnt and so damaging their ability to absorb water.
Also see Feeding tips

BATHE DRIED-OUT POTPLANTS

If you have allowed your potplant to dry out by mistake, and it is small enough to handle, immerse the entire pot in a container of water. Make sure that the top of the compost is under the water level. Once all the bubbles have risen to the top, the compost will be thoroughly wet through.

Also see Watering tips

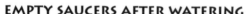

EMPTY SAUCERS AFTER WATERING

Never allow a pot to stand in a saucer filled with water. Once the pot has been watered and has been allowed to drain, the excess water must be removed from the saucer. If the pot is too heavy to lift, simply use a cloth and a bucket to mop up all the water in the saucer. If water is left in the saucer over a prolonged period, the plant could eventually drown. Plant roots are also deprived of the oxygen necessary for healthy development. In extreme circumstances, plant roots will start to rot.

Unless you really have to, avoid using saucers under pots that are standing outside. If you do have saucers under pots, you can always drill a little hole in the side of the saucer, insert a small copper or plastic pipe into the hole, seal around the edge with silicone and lead the pipe to where you want the water to drain. Obviously, try to cover the pipe so that it cannot be seen.

LEAVE SPACE FOR WATER

Always leave a sensible gap between the rim of the pot and the top of the compost level to allow for thorough watering.

KNOW WHEN AND HOW MUCH TO WATER

When watering container plants, add enough water to the pot so that water drains out freely from the bottom in a steady stream. Once the water starts running out, you know that the all the compost in the pot is wet through – saucers hamper this process, another reason they are not a good idea for outdoor containers but are unavoidable for indoor plants.

The water running out the bottom of the pot also helps prevent a build-up of insoluble salts that will burn the roots. With regular watering, the salts and nutrients in the compost are removed through a process known as leaching, so remember to fertilize container plants on a regular basis to replenish all these necessary elements. Most plants in containers will accept fertilizing on a monthly basis without feeling the effects of overfeeding.

CONTAINER TYPES

MAKE A NEW POT LOOK OLD

Age containers made from cement by sandpapering them lightly to roughen the surface. Keep them in a moist, shady place and paint the surface with liquid manure or organic liquid fertilizer. Moss and algae will soon grow on the surface of the pots and give them that wonderful old, used look.

MINIMIZE THE EVAPORATION

Plastic pots tend to dry out much slower than terracotta pots. However, for garden use, terracotta, concrete or ceramic pots are recommended over plastic pots – mostly from an aesthetic point of view, as they are more 'earthy' looking.

To prevent terracotta containers drying out too quickly, paint the inside of the pot with a non-toxic silicone sealant that cuts down on the amount of evaporation. Be careful not to block the drainage hole.

SOUND OUT THOSE POTS FIRST

When buying terracotta or ceramic pots, give them a good hard knock on their sides with your knuckles. If you hear a clear ringing sound, you know that the pot has no cracks. If the sound you get is dull or fuzzy, leave that one and take another – it probably has a hairline crack that you would not notice with the naked eye, but which would get worse with time and certainly with the added weight of the compost, plant and water in it.

STOP YOUR WOODEN BARREL ROTTING

When using wooden containers such as wine barrels, place them on small feet or on a deep layer of gravel so that the wood can dry out between waterings, otherwise it will rot away. Line wooden barrels with a layer of thick plastic sheeting to prevent the wood from rotting or discolouring due to water damage. You can also use a silicone- or bitumen-based sealant on the inside of wooden containers to waterproof them.

GROUP SIMILAR COLOURS AND STYLES

When grouping different pots together, try to use pots of the same or similar colour. This helps to deceive the eye and makes the pots disappear into the background, allowing the plants to be the focal point. Also, pots with similar styles or shapes look best when used together in groupings.

Also see Colour tips

STOP CRACKS EARLY

If a terracotta pot has developed a crack in it, prevent this from spreading by tying some wire around the rim of the pot or over the area where the crack has appeared, and tighten it. This is only a temporary measure but will save your pot from cracking any further or even breaking completely. Be sure to plant something in the pot that will hide the wire.

Cracked or chipped terracotta pots can also be repaired using car body filler. Check with your local motor workshop.

AGE CONCRETE EASILY

To give concrete statues and pots an instant look of old age, spread yoghurt liberally over them every few days. Keep them in a shady area in-between yoghurt applications until they turn a greenish colour. Concrete pots also take well to paint techniques and you can create wonderful-looking containers by using paint skilfully.

CHOOSE SIMPLE, OPEN-SHAPED POTS

Try to avoid using a pot that has a rim that is narrower than the rest of the body (Ali Baba-shaped). At a later stage, when it becomes necessary to repot the plant, the narrower opening will make removing the plant without damaging its roots an impossible task. The ideal pot has a slight 'V' or 'U' shape to the inside, making it an easy task to get any plant out.

If you do have a plant in a pot that is an awkward shape and you need to plant it out or repot it, make a decision about which is more valuable. If the plant gets your vote above the pot, the best thing to do is to break the pot. If the pot is more valuable than the plant, try turning it on its side and use a hose to wash out the compost that is in the pot, exposing the plant's roots. Now you can gently tug at them until they come out. If there is the odd root that is too big for the pot you can, if you really have to, cut it off. When replanting, be sure that you get the new compost in between all the roots without leaving any air pockets. Flood it with water to ensure that the compost particles are washed between all the roots, then top up the compost afterwards as it settles.

CUT FLOWERS

USE POTTED PLANTS AS CENTREPIECES

Potted plants used as centrepieces for special occasions can be much more satisfactory – and certainly less costly – than cut flowers. Little pots of plants can be given to the guests as souvenirs once the function has ended. At a wedding, for instance, a memento could take the form of a small pot of ivy, which is a symbol of fidelity, with a fresh flower from the bridal bouquet added – the ivy can later be planted in the recipient's garden to serve as a reminder of the occasion.

Potted plants will also last longer and are easier to keep alive than cut flowers. This is handy in that you can start your table arrangements or centrepieces long before the wedding and so reduce some of that last-minute pressure.

GIVE CUT FLOWERS A SECOND CHANCE

Cloudy and smelly water in the vase is a sure sign that the stems of the cut flowers are beginning to rot, or that bacteria is building up. Remedy this by emptying the container completely. Remove the leaves that have been under water and have become discoloured from the stems of the flowers, wash the stems well using fresh water, and wash out the vase well. Now refill the vase, add a cut flower feed, cut off the bottom of all the stems and replace them in the vase.

LOSE MORE LEAVES

Remove most of the leaves from the stems of cut flowers that are to be submerged in water. This will prevent decomposing leaves from fouling the water and making it smelly. It will also prevent the development of bacteria that might clog the stems and prevent water uptake.

CUT FLOWERS IN THE COOL

Cutting flowers from the garden is best done late in the afternoon. Failing this, the next best option is early in the morning. Once you have cut them, plunge the flowers right up to their necks in a deep, water-filled container. If you can manage to carry the bucket of water with you while cutting the flowers, so much the better. Store overnight in a cool, draught-free room before arranging.

AVOID TULIP DROOP

When arranging tulips in a vase, use only a little water in the bottom of the vase to prevent the tulip stems from becoming too waterlogged and flopping over. Adding cut flower feed to the water will also help to keep the stems firm and rigid.

FRESHEN UP SHOP-BOUGHT FLOWERS

When buying cut flowers from the florist, always re-cut the stems – preferably under water – when you get them home, before plunging them in a deep bucket of water for several hours before use.

PREVENT YELLOW POLLEN STAINS

If you happen to get pollen on your clothes whilst working with cut flowers such as lilies which have large pollen stamens, never try to remove it with a damp cloth. This causes the colour to run into the fibres of your clothing and makes it almost impossible to remove. If you have a vacuum cleaner handy, this is the best way to remove the pollen. Otherwise shake the piece of clothing or lightly brush off as much of the pollen as you can and then use sticky tape to remove the rest. It is easier to first remove the pollen stamens from the flower, if it has already opened, before you start arranging the flowers. Use a plastic or rubber kitchen glove, or even a piece of paper towel to do this and avoid the problem before it presents itself.

PLUNGE STEMS OF CUT ROSES INTO BOILING WATER

Place the bottom 3cm (1in) of cut roses into boiling water for three to four minutes and then plunge them into a bucket of cold water. This prevents an air bubble from forming in the stem and reducing the life of the flower.

USE OASIS CORRECTLY

When arranging cut flowers in oasis or florist's foam, make sure that you do not pull the stem out slightly once you have inserted it – this creates a gap below the base of the stem, which should be in contact with the foam to absorb water properly. By cutting the stem at an angle, you increase the area of absorption and can also wedge the stem in more firmly.

EXTEND THE LIFESPAN

When arranging flowers in a vase or in any container, add a teaspoon of household bleach per 1 litre (1³/₄ pints) of water. This prevents the stems from decomposing and clogging up the stem cells. It also prevents the formation of bacteria and will add days to the lifespan of cut flowers.

There are many cut flower feeds on the market which work incredibly well and can extend certain cut flowers' lifespans by up to three weeks. However, be warned: don't use them in metallic containers as the metal could discolour or even corrode.

Make your own cut flower feed with this easy recipe:

Per 1 litre (1³/₄ pints) of water for the vase, mix:

2 tsp sugar
1 tsp vinegar
1 aspirin

Dissolve the ingredients in a small amount of warm water and then add cold water. Fill the container with the mixture and arrange the flowers. You can even soak oasis foam in this mixture before using it and then top up the container using the same mixture.

PICK OPEN HYDRANGEAS

When cutting hydrangeas from the garden make sure that all the centre flowers on the flower head are open. If these flowers are still immature and closed the hydrangea will wilt and die too quickly. Place the cut hydrangea stems into 3cm (1in) of boiling water for three to four minutes before plunging them up to their necks in cool water and leaving them overnight.

Cuttings

USE ROOTING HORMONES

When taking cuttings of plants, always use a hormone rooting powder, available from your local nursery. There are specific and different compounds available for each type of plant, such as those with hard or soft wood. Buy according to the type of material you are making the cuttings from, or ask at your local nursery for advice as to which compound you need for your particular plant.

USE CLEAN PLANT MATERIAL

Never take cuttings from a plant that shows signs of having disease on it, such as scale, fungus or die-back. These diseases will lessen your chance of success. Similarly, always use clean sharp sand or potting compost that has not been used before, and never soil from the garden, as it contains certain organisms that might be harmful to the new cutting and might cause it to start rotting once planted.

A good mix to plant cuttings in is three parts clean sharp sand to one part potting compost. This will ensure fast drainage and prevent the cutting from being kept too wet. Otherwise, just use plain sharp sand. Always buy new, clean pots to grow cuttings in and never use seed trays or plastic pots that have contained other plants unless you have washed and sterilized them.

NEVER PUSH THE CUTTING INTO THE SAND

This will cause damage to the bark. Instead, make a big enough hole using a blunt instrument like the back of a pencil or a sawn-off piece of broom handle, place the cutting in the hole and cover loosely with the displaced sand. Press down well afterwards and keep moist, but not wet, until growth starts. Create your own miniature hothouse by loosely covering the cuttings with clear plastic, ensuring it is sealed at the bottom.

TAKE CUTTINGS AT THE CORRECT TIME OF THE YEAR

Depending on the plant itself and its type of wood, the general rules are:

- **Deciduous plants and hardwood cuttings** must be made when the plant is dormant in winter. These should be thick pieces of stem taken from plants like berberis, hydrangea, buddleja, cornus, photinia, pittosporum, spiraea and viburnum.
- **Leaf cuttings** are made in spring or summer from, for example, African violets, begonias and gloxinia.
- **Softwood cuttings** from the growing tip of the plant are also done in spring, for plants such as cotoneaster, fuchsia, ligustrum, forsythia, and philadelphus.
- **Semi-ripe cuttings** are best taken in summer, from plants such as aucuba, azalea, camellia, hibiscus, lavender and skimmia.

DIVISION

SPLIT PERENNIALS REGULARLY

Once perennials, such as agapanthus, hemerocallis, hostas, grasses and alstroemeria, have been growing in the garden for a few years, they tend to become very thick and need dividing and replanting. The best way is to dig out the entire plant with as many roots as possible. Take two garden forks and place them with their teeth back-to-back against each other into the centre of the plant, and force the handles apart. You will find that the plants separate quite easily. Continue doing this until you end up with a few plants bunched together, which you then replant.

To ensure regular flowering, divide perennials as soon as you see that the plant has become very large and as flowering declines. Perennials' side suckers are the flower-bearing parts of the plant, which is the reason to keep them young and multiplying. The best time is in early spring, just as you see the new foliage emerging.

Also see Perennials tips

FEEDING

ONLY APPLY FERTILIZER TO WET SOIL

Always ensure that the ground is wet before applying any form of fertilizer. Once applied, water it in well. If the soil is too dry, the fertilizer will be absorbed too quickly by the roots, leading to fertilizer burn, which can kill the plant entirely or set it back so badly that it might never recover. This applies to both chemical and organic fertilizer products.

USE WELL-MATURED ORGANIC FERTILIZERS

Organic fertilizers, derived from plant and/or animal products like manure, seaweed or bone meal, are much safer to use in dry conditions but also need water to activate them in the soil. Only ever use manure once it has been well rotted and is very old – six months at least – otherwise it will burn the roots of the plants. (Fresh manure contains large amounts of ammonia.)
Also see Organic Alternatives tips

OPT FOR LIQUID ORGANIC FERTILIZERS FOR EASE-OF-USE

Good organic liquid fertilizers make it difficult to burn or overfeed your plants. Liquid forms of fertilizer are very easily absorbed by plant roots and leaves and are easy to apply with a sprayer or watering can. When using foliar feeds, be sure to apply them when there is no presence of rain or before watering the garden. This will avoid the fertilizer being washed off the plant leaves. This also means that the fertilizer will be absorbed by the roots as opposed to the leaves and so won't go to waste, but roots don't absorb fertilizer as quickly as leaves do.

PREVENT YELLOW LEAVES

If, despite ideal growing conditions, your plants are showing signs of yellowing leaves, they are probably lacking trace elements from the soil. Apply a foliar feed product which contains micronutrients such as boron, zinc, molybdenum, copper and manganese – all vital for healthy plant growth. These trace elements are available in such small quantities in the soil that they can leach out very quickly and need to be replaced regularly. If you are not sure of the exact problem, take a few leaves to your nursery and they will quickly be able to tell whether the plant lacks these micronutrients.

Yellow leaves can also be a result of the plant being short of iron. In this case, use the iron products available from garden shops or sprinkle iron filings around the plant. These will rust and the resulting powder is then washed into the soil to become available to the plant's roots. Plants requiring large amounts of iron include azaleas, camellias, citrus trees and gardenias.

FERTILIZER SAFETY

Fertilizers can be harmful chemicals so treat them with respect. Always follow the manufacturer's instructions to the letter and do not attempt to mix them with any other product. Always keep them in their original bottles so nobody is in any doubt as to what they are. Wear gloves when handling fertilizers and avoid breathing in their dust or spray. Keep all garden chemicals away from children.

MULCH ACID LOVERS WITH PINE NEEDLES

Because pine needles are very acid, they make excellent mulch or compost for acid-loving plants like azaleas, blue hydrangeas, camellias and rhododendrons.
Also see Mulching tips

DON'T BOOST PLANT GROWTH TOO LATE IN AUTUMN

Do not feed the garden too late in the autumn as this will encourage soft growth that might be damaged by early frosts or cold weather. For the same reason, when planting winter annuals and bulbs, apply compost and fertilizer only to the selected area where these plants are to be grown.

ACHIEVE THE CORRECT SPREAD

If the instructions on the bag of fertilizer suggest a quantity to be applied per square metre, do the following: Stick a few sheets of newspaper together and cut the paper to exactly one square metre. Lay the square down on the lawn. Place a small weight on each corner to prevent it moving. Set your fertilizer spreader to the setting that you think will be most suitable. Start pushing the spreader over the newspaper square on the lawn. Once the spreader has moved over the square, lift the paper and carefully transfer the collected fertilizer into the bowl of your scales and measure the exact weight. You can now adjust the size of your fertilizer spreader's holes, depending on the results obtained from the scales.

GIVE VINEGAR TO ACID LOVERS

Azaleas, rhododendrons and camellias need an acid soil, and you may have a problem with leaves yellowing if you live in a hardwater area. Add two tablespoons of vinegar to 1 litre (1 3/4 pints) of water and pour this around the base of the plants. Repeat every three weeks until the leaves are green and healthy.

DON'T FERTILIZE WEAK PLANTS

Do not try to feed a plant that is under any form of stress, for example one that has recently been replanted, overwatered or endured drought conditions.

Just keep the plant reasonably well watered until it recovers before adding any fertilizer to the soil. When a plant's leaves and stems have dried out too much, it might need a light pruning to encourage it to start shooting – only then should you apply fertilizer. Do, however, include compost in the hole when transplanting, and avoid using chemical fertilizers.

KNOW YOUR FUSSY FEEDERS

Azaleas and camellias resent having artificial fertilizers dug in around their root systems and will not respond to the treatment. Instead use an organic liquid fertilizer to foliar feed them, as plants absorb nutrients through their leaves as well as through their roots. Peat or acid composts, or even pine needles, are useful for mulching these plants as they are acid-loving. Certain deficiencies can be corrected by using seaweed concentrates as foliar feeds but these should be seen as supplementary to chemical fertilizers to correct the following deficiencies: nitrogen (yellowing leaves); potassium (yellow leaf edges and mottling); phosphorous (purple, stressed-looking leaves and stunted growth).

MAKE YOUR OWN COMPOST

Garden compost makes a great feed and mulch for all sorts of plants, and what's more it's free. To make your own compost heap, pile up layers of nitrogen-rich materials, such as grass clippings and soft weeds, and carbon-rich materials, such as bark and newspaper. Almost any plant matter and kitchen waste can be composted, but avoid any cooked matter which will attract rats, and any plant seedheads or pernicious weed roots which will regrow. Turn the pile from time to time to mix up the contents and let in some air. The compost is ready when it is brown, crumbly and sweet smelling.

FRAGRANT PLANTS

MAXIMIZE THE SCENT

Use fragrant flowering plants in enclosed areas such as courtyards, where the scent will be intensified as it is not dispersed by a breeze all the time. Plant fragrant plants close to the house or near windows to allow the whole house to be scented.

ENJOY NATURAL DRIED FLOWER FRAGRANCE

Cut blooms from scented roses and place them in a brown paper bag to dry out. When they have dried, add a few drops of rose oil and place the blooms and petals in a bowl to fill the room with a lovely natural fragrance.

FROST

CREATE A MINI-CLIMATE IN WHICH TO GROW TENDER PLANTS

If you are in an area that gets severe frost and you insist on having one of those very tender or frost-sensitive 'must haves' like a tree fern, orange tree or oleander, then plant it in a container and place the pot where there is less chance of being damaged by the cold, such as on a patio or a covered terrace. In this way you create a mini-climate for the plant to grow in and can take it under cover when frost is forecast. When passion for a plant overtakes your rational thinking, this is one way of ensuring that you can have the plant you always wanted but could never grow.
Also see Container Gardening tips

SPRAY WATER ON PLANTS COVERED WITH FROST

If your plants have a layer of frost on them, water them early in the morning with a fine mist spray before the sun gets to them. This will melt the ice and warm the leaves up gradually.

LEAVE FROST DAMAGE IN SITU

Do not be too over-eager to tidy frost-damaged plants by cutting them back or removing the damaged parts, as this can lead to more damage. Instead, leave the damaged parts on the plant to protect what remains. Wait until spring approaches and the plant starts to produce new shoots before cutting back the damaged part of the plant to where the new shoots are appearing.

FRUIT TREES

PREVENT DISEASE SPREADING

Sterilize pruning tools after each tree has been pruned by dipping them in household bleach or wiping them with methylated spirits. This helps to prevent diseases such as bacterial canker, a disease that fruit trees are prone to, spreading from tree to tree.

Also see Tools tips

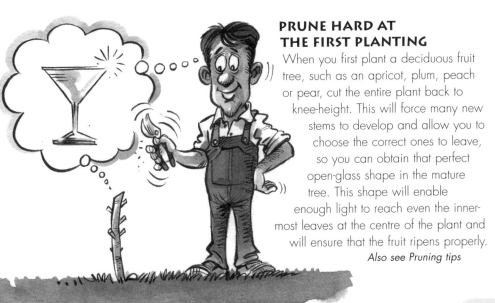

PRUNE HARD AT THE FIRST PLANTING

When you first plant a deciduous fruit tree, such as an apricot, plum, peach or pear, cut the entire plant back to knee-height. This will force many new stems to develop and allow you to choose the correct ones to leave, so you can obtain that perfect open-glass shape in the mature tree. This shape will enable enough light to reach even the inner-most leaves at the centre of the plant and will ensure that the fruit ripens properly.

Also see Pruning tips

DON'T KILL THE WORKERS

Never spray fruit trees while they are still in bloom. This would kill off insects or bees that are pollinating the flowers which are necessary for the fruit to develop. Without these insects and bees, your flowers will never be pollinated and the fruit will never form. Only start your spraying programme once the petals of the flowers start to drop off and the fruit is about the size of a pea.

KEEP PLUMS AND CHERRIES SAFE FROM SILVERLEAF

Plum and cherry trees are susceptible to silverleaf, so delay pruning them until the summer when the disease is less likely to attack. This disease causes the leaves to go silver, and gradually spreads from one branch to the next. If you come across the disease, cut back affected branches to 15cm (6in) below the affected wood which will have a central dark stain.

GRAVEL

USE GRAVEL FOR LOW MAINTENANCE

The use of gravel for pathways, driveways or in beds in level areas can cut down maintenance and reduce weeds. Gravel also allows rainwater to seep into the ground far more freely than does a hard, impenetrable surface like brick paving. If gravel is used on uneven ground, however, it will wash away in heavy downpours and even the scuffing action of feet and shoes will remove it from the higher areas.

When planting in areas where gravel is to be spread, first plant the plant, firm the soil down around it and then spread the gravel right up to the stem. Make sure that the gravel is at least 3cm (1in) thick when spreading. Remember to lift the plant's roots 3cm (1in) higher than the surrounding earth so that the crown of the plant is not lower than the finished level of the gravel. In this way you prevent it being covered by gravel in heavy downpours, which could result in a rotting stem.

USE THE SECURITY SMARTLY

Gravel used in pathways and on driveways is an excellent intruder deterrent as it makes that distinctive crunching sound when it is walked on, alerting you when someone approaches.

USE PLASTIC SHEETING UNDER GRAVEL

When making a gravel pathway, place plastic sheeting underneath the gravel to stop weeds growing through. (Remember to make some holes in the plastic to allow free drainage of water.) The plastic will also prevent the gravel mixing with the soil beneath, making it look unsightly.

GROUNDCOVER

KNOW THE GROWTH SPEED

Plant groundcover that will not run too rampant, as they could kill desired plants in the garden. But go ahead and use very rampant growing types if you are trying to cover areas such as steep banks where no lawn is to be planted, especially where the soil needs to be retained to prevent soil erosion.

Fast-spreading groundcover include *Ajuga reptans*, lamium and vinca. Slow-spreading groundcover include convolvulus, euonymus, nepeta, ophiopogon, stachys and thyme.

SPACE PLANTS CORRECTLY

When first planting groundcover, don't plant them too close together. Instead, use an organic mulch to cover the soil and allow the groundcover to grow in their own time. This saves money on buying plants and allows the plants to grow and establish themselves at their natural height and size and so reach their full potential. Once the groundcover have covered the soil fully, spread fertilizer over them and just water it in. Alternatively, use a liquid fertilizer to feed the garden.

HANGING BASKETS

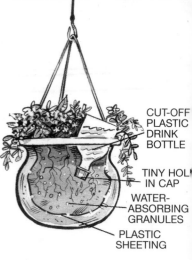

CUT-OFF
PLASTIC
DRINK
BOTTLE

TINY HOLE
IN CAP

WATER-
ABSORBING
GRANULES

PLASTIC
SHEETING

LINE HANGING BASKETS WITH PLASTIC

When planting a hanging basket, use a lining of plastic sheeting (such as a supermarket shopping bag) between the moss and the compost to prevent the compost from drying out too quickly. Be sure to punch some holes in the plastic before planting.

USE GRANULES IN THE POTTING MIX

Water-absorbing granules, available from garden centres, absorb large amounts of water and release it slowly. Adding these to the potting mix helps the compost stay wet for longer periods between waterings, but be careful of overwatering the plants and killing them with kindness.

GIVE THE BASKET A BOTTLE

You can provide a continuous water supply by inserting a cut-off plastic drink bottle, turned upside down, in the middle of a hanging basket. Make tiny holes in the cap using a heated piece of wire or a needle. The bottle acts as a water reservoir and releases water slowly over a period of time. Keep checking that the holes do not become blocked by debris that may be blown into the bottle.

DON'T HANG BASKETS TOO HIGH

By hanging them lower, you will have a better view of the plants and flowers and the ugly bottom of the basket won't be so visible. Try hanging baskets at eye level or even lower for best effect, applying the same principle to window boxes.

OPT FOR SHADE

Hanging baskets are generally better in lightly shaded positions – they tend to dry out very quickly if they are in the sun. If you do hang a basket in a sunny position, use drought-tolerant plants such as petunias, lobelia, geraniums, nasturtiums or any varieties that tolerate or even thrive in the heat.

HEDGES

CHOOSE THE CORRECT TYPE OF PLANT

Remember when planting hedges to choose a plant variety that does not grow too high or too vigorously. Opt for slower-growing varieties as these need less frequent cutting and keep their shape longer between clippings. Evergreen plants give you maximum screening and will ensure maximum privacy all year round, in contrast to deciduous plants that are bare in winter.

- **For formal hedges** choose box, yew, *Lonicera nitida*, escallonia, hawthorn, holly, privet or beech.
- **For informal hedges** choose berberis, cotoneaster, pyracantha, shrub roses, *Fuchsia magellanica* or *Garrya elliptica*.

PRUNE TO FORM A-SHAPED HEDGES

When pruning or trimming hedges, avoid doing so in such a way that you end up with the bottom of the hedge narrower than the top. The lower branches will then be in shade and may also never shoot out again. The ideal shape for a hedge is the shape of an 'A' so that the lower sections receive as much light as the top.

Also see Pruning tips

PRUNE HEDGING PLANTS HARD WHEN YOU FIRST PLANT THEM

This will encourage growth of the bottom branches and ensure you avoid see-through gaps forming along the base of the hedge. The hard pruning will encourage side branches to develop from as close to the ground as possible.

LOOK OUT FOR SUN AND SHADE VARIATIONS

If you are planting a hedge and it runs from a full sun position into a shady area along the same line, buy varieties that are happy to grow in both shade and sun positions. Examples include holly, yew and box.

HERBS

KEEP HERBS CLOSE TO THE KITCHEN

You know the old adage 'Out of sight, out of mind,' so if at all possible grow your herb garden as close to the kitchen as practical to make it quick and easy to pop out and pick the appropriate herbs. Bear in mind, however, that most herbs do prefer to be planted in full sun in well-drained soil to which lots of organic material has been added. They also like to be kept well watered.

GROW HERBS FROM SEED

Most herbs can be grown very successfully from seed. There are of course certain varieties that require vegetative propagation. Examples include most of the mint varieties and French tarragon, for which you have to split the original plant and remove some of it with roots attached, or make cuttings which have to be rooted first, preferably in sharp sand and then planted out once established.
Also see Seed Sowing tips

GO EASY ON THE QUANTITY

A herb such as rosemary is not used that frequently or in great quantities, so you will probably need only one plant for the average household. Basil, parsley, chives and others you might need in large quantities can then be given the extra space.

DON'T HARVEST TOO MUCH

Only pick what you need or will use that day, as herbs tend to lose their aromatic qualities when stored for too long. Do not strip the entire plant of its leaves at any one time – leave enough to sustain the plant until you harvest again. Also try to pick herbs early in the day as that is when they have the most aroma in their leaves.

USE HERBS AS INSECT REPELLENTS

Apart from their many culinary uses, some herbs and related plants make excellent insect repellents. Examples include garlic, chives, basil and rue. These give off odours that are disliked by insects and are an ideal way to cut down on the amount of chemical insecticide used in the garden – especially in the vegetable plot, where some of these chemicals could be very harmful to human health.

You can also make your own insecticide by using herbs like garlic to deter sucking and chewing insects. The list of herbs that are useful as insect repellents and in companion planting is vast, so it is worth investing in a specialized book on this subject.

Also see Pests & Diseases tips

PRUNE EVERGREEN HERBS

Cut back perennial herbs like thyme, marjoram, chives, borage, basil, rosemary and all the mints in early spring to encourage new growth. Save the cut leaves for use either by placing them in small packets and freezing or by drying in the shade and storing in airtight containers.

CUT DOWN ON FERTILIZER

Keep fertilizing to a minimum in the herb garden. Over-fertilizing promotes lush foliage at the expense of taste and aroma.

Also see Feeding tips

KEEP MINT UNDER CONTROL

To prevent mint taking over your entire herb garden, sink it in a pot in the ground – watch that the pot is not too deep or the mint will merely send runners over the top, defeating the point. Mint is also less aggressive in the shade.

HOUSE PLANTS

DON'T OVERWATER

Water less frequently but more thoroughly. People tend to overwater their potplants, causing them to rot and die. In fact, more potplants die from overwatering than any other cause. If a plant looks wilted, don't water before you've checked the soil moisture in the pot by sticking your finger in around the edge. If it is really dry and needs water, go ahead, but if it is still damp or wet, leave it to dry out – the wilting is probably caused by the plant being too wet, either from overwatering or from standing in a full saucer. Once watered, never leave indoor plants standing in trays of water – excess water must be poured off as soon as possible.

Also see Container Plants –
Feeding & Watering tips

CLEAN THE LEAVES REGULARLY

Use a mixture of milk, water and a soft cloth to wipe down indoor plants' leaves and give them a gloss. Regularly remove dust build-up on the leaves to prevent the pores from clogging up. This also allows more light to hit the surface of the plant which is essential for photosynthesis to occur and the necessary nutrients to be manufactured.

FEED INDOOR PLANTS APPROPRIATELY

Plants bought from a nursery should not need feeding for at least three months. However, you should feed indoor plants regularly during the growing season as they cannot send out their roots to find their own food and therefore easily become starved of nutrients. Any food available in the compost gets leached out with regular watering so ensure that it is replaced by regular feeding.

There is a host of potplant fertilizers to choose from, and it is important to follow their instructions for use carefully. Too little is better than too much. Do not feed sick plants, newly-potted plants or those that are dry or dormant.

LOOK OUT FOR SMALLER LEAVES

Check if the new leaves formed by an indoor plant are smaller than the previous ones. This is a sign that the plant is being starved of nutrients and needs to be repotted. By regularly feeding or repotting the plant, the problem should disappear.
Also see Feeding and Planting & Transplanting tips

SUIT THE PLANT TO THE LIGHTING

Before buying indoor plants be sure to seek expert advice on the selection of the correct plant for the situation you have in mind. As a general rule, if it is a dimly lit area, then buy a plant that will tolerate low light intensity, such as *Aspidistra*, *Aglaonema* or *Sanseveria*. Plants with dark green foliage will often survive better in low light and those with lighter or variegated foliage require more light. In a dimly lit room, rotate the plant regularly to avoid all the leaves growing towards the light. Never place house plants in a draught – they hate it and will not do well.

GET PERFECT AIR CIRCULATION TO AVOID INSECTS

If any of the insects listed below appear on your indoor plant, take that as a certain indication of a lack of air circulation in the room in which the plant is growing. Open windows or doors to relieve the problem, but remember too that indoor plants do not like draughty areas.

● **Mealy bug** – a small, greyish-brown, sucking insect. To get rid of it, soak cotton wool in a mixture of half water and half methylated spirits and wipe the insect off the plant.

● **Scale** – a small, hard, brown insect, which appears on the stems of plants. To kill this you need to spray the plant with a product which has an oil base that suffocates the pest.

● **Woolly aphid** – a small, white, fluffy insect, which looks like a lump of cotton wool, usually found on the stems of indoor plants. To remove it, dip a soft cloth into a solution of half water and half methylated spirits and wipe the insect gently with the cloth to kill it.

If you don't object to chemical insecticides, use a systemic poison and water it into the soil around the plant. The poison gets taken up into the stem and, as insects suck the sap, they ingest the poison and die.

Also see Pests & Diseases tips

MAXIMIZE ORCHID LIGHT AND HUMIDITY

Greenhouse-grown orchids must only be brought inside once the *first* flower on the flower spike has opened. If brought in too early, the flowers will not open properly, especially if they find themselves in a position with low light. Most orchids' flowers last for a very long time so place them in a very bright part of the room to enable them to continue growing properly whilst being used for indoor display.

Stand orchid plants on a bed of gravel placed in a water-filled tray, ensuring that the bottom of the pot is not in direct contact with the water as this might lead to overwatering. The idea is to increase the humidity around the orchid, especially for the more tropical varieties of orchids like the *Cattleya* and *Phalaenopsis*, though this is not necessary for *Cymbidium* species.

SET UP A DRINKING SYSTEM

If you are going away for a short while, water your house plants thoroughly and place their containers flat on a super-absorbent matting, a geotextile fibre available from most nurseries. Let the end of the matting hang into a basin filled with water – the kitchen sink is probably your best bet. As the plants use up the water in the pot, the water from the sink will be drawn up by the fibre and find its way into the pot through capillary action.

ABSORBENT MATTING

41

LAWNS

USE GROUNDCOVER TO REDUCE MOWING

Use low-growing, hardy groundcover instead of grass to cut down on the weekly task of mowing large areas of lawn.

Also see Groundcover tips

SPRING BOOST

Just like any other plants, grasses need nutrients to grow. A spring feed will give your lawn a boost, making it grow thicker and lusher. Apply a proprietary lawn feed just before rain is forecast. Most of the products come as granules which are simply sprinkled on the lawn, and many also contain a weedkiller to remove undesirables at the same time.

MAKE MOWING EASIER

- Keep objects like **benches, birdbaths, pots and furniture** off the lawn areas and place them on paved areas or anywhere you are not mowing grass.
- When you are constructing beds in the garden, remember that **curved corners** in the lawn are easier to mow than right-angled ones. The shape of the bed must, however, obviously be determined by the overall design of the garden.
- In a very large lawn consider creating **a group planting** with trees surrounded by different varieties of grasses or groundcovers. In other words, simply make a bed in the middle of your lawn, which will create a meadow-type effect and cut down on the amount of mowing needed.
- Don't let your lawn be an obstacle course for the lawnmower. Keep lawn areas uncluttered and **beds towards the edges** of the property.
- Make your **grass pathways** between beds at least 1m (3ft) wide for easier mowing.

CREATE A MOWING STRIP

Construct **a mowing strip or edging strip** along the edges of your lawn where it meets the garden beds to make the maintenance of the edges much easier. You can use things like bricks laid in cement, short wooden poles either laid on their sides or knocked into the ground, strips of stainless steel or aluminium laid on their sides or any material that will not move once it is in place. Keep it to the same level as your lawn and you can simply run the lawnmower slightly over the edging strip to make sure that you mow even the very edge of the lawn.

Solid edging around the lawn will maintain the shape and position of its borders and prevent the edges from becoming wavy and uneven, and it also provides a means of keeping the grass contained. If the material you construct the edge with goes deep enough, it will even prevent grass growing into the beds and having to be dug out regularly.

AVOID SMALL AREAS OF LAWN

In small areas, use hard landscaping materials like gravel, bark chips or brick paving instead of lawn. A small lawn is difficult to maintain, especially where it must endure heavy traffic – a common scenario in townhouses or small courtyards. Grass pathways are also a bad idea – the concentrated wear tends to make unsightly bald patches.

TURF OR SEED?

When planning a new lawn, you have the choice of laying turf or sowing seed. Seed is the cheaper option but it will take longer to establish. Turf is much more expensive but you will have an instant lawn.

WHEN TO MOW

Start regular mowing in spring when the lawn has started to grow. Choose a period of warm, dry weather and set the blades to high for the first few cuts. Thereafter the frequency of mowing and the height of the blades depends on the lawn's rate of growth.

AERATE LAWNS

Scarify and aerate lawns in autumn to encourage deep root growth and remove thatch. Aeration of the lawn also allows extra oxygen to enter the soil for healthy root development. If you have a large area, hire a machine. Small lawns can be raked and spiked by hand.

USE YOUR LAWNMOWER AS A VACUUM CLEANER

Instead of spending hours raking leaves, let the lawnmower do the job for you. Unless you need to cut the grass at the same time, set the blades on high and allow the lawnmower to 'vacuum clean' any debris into its grass box. This not only ensures that you pick up all the fallen leaves, but the blades of the lawnmower will shred the leaves into finer pieces and they will in turn become compost more quickly.

MULCH AS YOU MOW

There are lawnmowers on the market nowadays that will turn the grass clippings into a mulch as you mow. As you cut the grass, the mulching action takes place with the grass clippings forced into and under the lawn surface. This saves on having to use a grass catcher or raking the cut grass afterwards, making life a lot easier and avoiding the unsightly dead grass clippings that are inevitably scattered about.
Also see Tools tips

LAWNS IN SHADY AREAS

Choose a suitable grass type when creating a lawn in a shady area. Both turf and grass seed mixtures can be bought specially designed for shade. If the shade is very deep, use a ground cover plant instead as no grasses will thrive there. Plants such as ivy and ajuga will cover the ground quickly and require little care.
Also see Groundcover tips

GO EASY ON GRASSES PLANTED FROM SEED

The roots of recently sown grasses are not as strong as those of turf, so take care when mowing. Set the blades on high until the lawn is well established.

REPAIRING A DAMAGED EDGE

Unsupported lawn edges are especially vulnerable to damage and difficult to repair. If the edge of the lawn has fallen away or there is a bald patch, lift a square of turf around the damaged section. Turn the turf around and replace it so the damaged area is now inside the lawn and the lawn edge is perfect once more. Simply fill the bald patch with a little sandy soil and sprinkle with some grass seed.

OIL MOWER BLADES IN THE WET

Mowing wet grass is a risky business and should be avoided if at all possible. However, if it is necessary to mow dew-covered or rain-damp grass, wipe the blades with vegetable (sunflower) oil to prevent the wet grass clippings from sticking to them.

MULCHING

There are many different types of material that may be used for mulching but the purpose is usually one or more of the following: to improve the quality of the soil, prevent weeds growing, conserve moisture, or cover the surface of the soil in areas where there are no plants or beds.

There are two basic types of mulch:

● **Organic materials** in the form of garden compost, leafmould, bark chips, well-rotted manure and straw. These are usually used in garden beds.

● **Non-organic materials** include gravel and stone chips, as well as mulch fabric. These fabrics are most commonly used under gravel and stones on pathways.

USE CHEAP MULCHES

Go ahead and use the cheapest material that you can find to do the job that needs to be done.

USE MATERIALS THAT ALLOW WATER TO SOAK THROUGH

Avoid anything that will form an impenetrable 'thatch' that prevents water from entering the ground, as grass clippings often do. Variation in the size of the particles making up the mulch is usually a guarantee that it will remain porous and friable. Another good preventative measure is to ensure that the soil underneath is wet before any mulch is added to the surface.

REGULATE SOIL TEMPERATURE WITH MULCHES

To keep the soil temperature warmer in winter and help prevent frost damage, make use of thick layers of mulch, which conversely also help to reduce the soil temperature in summer. Apply mulches as thickly as possible to keep moisture in the soil.

KEEP MULCH MOIST

Mulches must be kept moist at all times as they play host to thousands of insects and worms that sustain bird life in the garden, as well as the millions of microbes that work to break down organic material. Moisture encourages this microbial activity and so speeds up the breaking-down process.

ADD MULCH TO EASE WEEDING

Weeds that do grow through the mulch cover are usually not well rooted and are easier to pull out by hand.

BARK CHIPS

PLASTIC SHEETING

STOP MUD AND DIRT SPLASHES

To prevent soil splashing onto plants as you water or during a downpour, place leafmould or plastic sheeting around the plants, hiding the latter under bark chips.

APPLY FERTILIZER WHEN MULCHING

Organic mulches do not necessarily feed the soil, so extra food in the form of fertilizer or manure must still be applied. It is advisable to sprinkle this on before you apply the mulch at the beginning of the season. For best results, apply your mulch in spring before the heat of summer arrives, and follow with a top-up in autumn.

Also see Feeding tips

DON'T LET MULCHES ROT PLANT STEMS

Keep mulch away from plant stems as it can cause the bark on the stem to remain too moist, thereby damaging it – once the bark of a plant dies, the entire plant will be lost.

SAVE EFFORT AND USE LEAVES TO MULCH

A thick layer of raked leaves makes a good mulch in shrub borders. Over time the leaves decompose, acting as your very own compost heap without your having to pile them up and turn them regularly. The layer also becomes a haven for insects and worms that will feed the birds. Simply rake fallen leaves directly into the beds where they are needed, rather than removing them to the compost heap, waiting for them to decompose and then bringing them all the way back again.

Also see Feeding tips

ORGANIC ALTERNATIVES

KEEP COMPOST HEAPS FRIABLE AND OXYGENATED

Prevent the compost heap from becoming too dense by incorporating bulky ingredients like twigs and small branches into the pile. When making compost, remember that the decomposition process of organic materials requires oxygen, so make the compost heap above ground and not in a hole – you want the maximum amount of oxygen to reach the decomposing material. Also, by making it in a hole you run the risk of rain and garden water running in and leaving you with a hole full of rotting smelly material that is useless for use at a later stage.

KEEP IT HOT

Compost heaps are also most effective in sunny areas where the temperature can increase and speed up the process of decomposition. Enough heat, and even weeds and harmful bacteria will be killed off.

SANDWICH WITH SOIL LAYERS

Use organic material in layers, with garden soil in between, to add more of the vital microbes that are needed as catalysts for the composting process. Animal manure also introduces nutrients and microbes.

ACCELERATE THE DECOMPOSITION PROCESS

Use a compost accelerator, sold at most nurseries, to speed up the breaking down of plant material. Bought as a dry powder, this is mixed with lukewarm water and sprinkled onto the compost heap. The accelerator contains millions of microbes that, once hydrated, become active and start to work away at breaking down the organic material. Compost accelerators can speed up the process by as much as fifty percent.

CALL IN THE WORMS

Go ahead and water your heap – microbes, earthworms and other breakdown-assisting creatures will only survive in moist areas and you need all the help you can get for the job of breaking down the solid matter in the heap.

TURN THE HEAP OFTEN

By turning the inside matter to the outside, you expose the organic material to the oxygen so vital for decomposition. Microbes need this element in order to function properly.

USE DRIED EARTHWORM CASINGS AS A CONDITIONER

Earthworm casings sold in dried form at most nurseries are excellent for use in the garden as they are full of nutrients and make excellent soil conditioners. You can also use them to sprinkle in the compost heap as you build it up.

GIVE THE NEW HEAP A HEAD START

Sift the compost before use and use all the matter that did not pass through the sieve as the starting layer for your next heap.

NEVER APPLY FRESH MANURE TO ANY PLANT

Manure contains large amounts of ammonia that will burn and kill plant roots. If you are lucky enough to have a supply of chicken or horse manure at hand, first compost it for at least six months before using it. Buying manure in bags from your local nursery is a safe alternative that is ready for immediate use.

USING GRASS CLIPPINGS AS COMPOST MATERIAL

Unless you have mixed lawn clippings with other materials, they can form a dense impenetrable mass in the compost heap. Mix them with leaves, twigs or anything with a bit of bulk.

USE GARLIC AS AN ORGANIC INSECTICIDE

For use against chewing and sucking insects, make your own spray by crushing five large cloves of garlic very finely. Add 1 litre (1 3/4 pints) of boiling water and, when cool, add another 4 litres (7 pints) of cold water. Another alternative is to use two teacups of finely chopped rhubarb leaves soaked overnight in 5 litres (9 pints) of water.

USE MILK TO PREVENT FUNGUS DISEASES ON ROSES

Spray rose bushes with undiluted full cream milk to stop mildew and fungal diseases.

USE BOILING WATER AS A WEEDKILLER

Instead of using commercial weedkillers on your paving areas, try boiling salt water. Pour this onto the plants and they will soon wilt and die.

PERENNIALS

DIVIDE NEW PLANTS WHEN YOU BUY THEM

When buying perennials in the nursery, look for plants that are very well established and seem almost to overfill the containers they are in. When you get them home you will be able to divide these plants up and cover an area twice the size of the one you would have covered with single small plants.

Also see Division tips

USE PERENNIALS RATHER THAN ANNUALS

Instead of relying on annuals to give colour in the garden, use flowering perennial plants or groundcovers. This cuts down on a lot of work as annuals need to be replaced at least twice a year and perennials last for many years.

PESTICIDES & POISONS

CHOOSE BY ACTIVE INGREDIENT

When purchasing pesticides or fungicides, don't just look for a product name but find out its active ingredient to establish whether you don't already have something similar in your poison cupboard.

STICK TO RECOMMENDED DOSAGES

A stronger pesticide mix will not do the job any faster and a weaker mix might help the pest become immune to the chemical you are using to kill it.

DON'T MIX BOTTLES

Never pour an insecticide into any bottle other than the one it came in, especially not a bottle in which the contents were meant for human consumption. Keep containers you mix pesticides in separate, and keep all insecticides locked away to prevent children or animals getting to them. If you have to put the insecticide in another bottle, be sure to carefully label it – and not with water-soluble ink as you might spill some of the liquid down the side of the bottle and over the writing.

PLAY IT SAFE

● **Wash your hands in cold water** with ordinary household soap after working with pesticides. While hot water might seem the better option, it would open the pores and could allow pesticide residues to penetrate the skin.

● When using pesticide sprays, **avoid harming beneficial insects** whenever possible. Honeybees, as a rule, do not forage at dawn or dusk and this is therefore a good time for application on flowering plants.

● **Strictly observe the waiting period,** as specified on the label, between the last application of a pesticide and the harvesting of treated fruit or vegetables.

● **Wash all equipment** thoroughly.

● If you feel nauseous, have a headache, or feel unwell after working with pesticides, **call your doctor** immediately and give them your symptoms as well as the active ingredients contained in the pesticide you were using.

THE TYPES OF CHEMICALS

Pesticides are used to kill insects, mites and other pests, while fungicides are used to control fungal diseases. Both types can work by either being brought into direct contact with the pest, or by being systemic. Contact pesticides kill pests when they crawl over a treated surface or are sprayed with the chemical directly. Systemic pesticides are absorbed into the plant tissues and kill pests as they try to eat the plant, or fungi within the plant.

SPRAY LATE IN THE AFTERNOON

Some insecticides are manufactured with an oil base that will stick to the leaves, so always spray late in the afternoon to prevent sun damage.

MIX ONLY THE REQUIRED AMOUNT

When making up pesticides, mix only the exact amount required. Once mixed, all of it must be used immediately – you should not keep mixed solutions for use on another day. If you have mixed too much, don't throw it down a drain to get rid of the excess as this would poison the water system. Rather dig a deep hole in the garden and pour the mix into it, or continue spraying until all the solution is used up.

PESTS & DISEASES

ANTS: CHASE THEM OFF WITH TANSY & LEMON

● The presence of ants in the garden is usually a sign of dry, sandy soil. If you have an ant problem, work in lots of **organic material** and keep the area well watered. Ants hate moist soil and will soon disappear.

● To keep ants at bay, plant **tansy** (*Tanacetum vulgare*) as a foundation plant around the house or around any other area where ants are a nuisance. Dried tansy, crushed and sprinkled in cupboards, is often used as an ant repellent. Strategically placed sprigs of the plant can be used to keep ants out of dog bowls – it seems the ants do not like to walk across the plant.

● Ants also dislike **lemon**. Pour the juice down their holes and put some of the rind in the hole or near affected plants. The ants will not pass over or near the lemon rind.

DON'T KILL THEM ALL

Not all insects and other creatures found in the garden are there to damage your plants. Some will actually help by preying on other insect pests or pollinating your flowers. For example, ladybird larvae feed on aphids, while centipedes are voracious hunters which prey on many soil-borne pests. Bees and hoverflies are great pollinators and should be encouraged. Take great care when using pesticides to only target the problem species.

ENCOURAGE THE GOOD GUYS

Hedgehogs, birds, frogs and toads can all help in the garden as they eat many plant pests, including slugs, snails and aphids. Encourage these beneficial creatures by providing food, water, hiding places and somewhere for them to breed.

BEWARE OF SPRAY DRIFT

Never spray in windy conditions – you don't want spray drifting onto other plants or coming into contact with your skin or eyes.

EELWORM: BURN THE PLANTS

Eelworms are tiny hard-to-see organisms which infest plant roots where they use the nutrients produced by the host plant and cause irreparable damage and even the death of the plant. A tell-tale sign of the presence of eelworms is when your plants suddenly get smaller and smaller and appear to be stunted. Also look for tiny malformed nodules on the roots that can be seen easily if you remove the plant from the soil.

Eelworm cannot resist invading the roots of marigolds (*Tagetes*), so if you suspect you have eelworm in your soil, plant a crop of marigolds. When these have finished flowering, pull them up and burn the plants or place them in the rubbish bag for removal. Do the same for any plant found to have eelworms on its roots. Under no circumstances place the plant on your compost heap, from where the pest can simply find its way back into the garden or infest a new area. Do not use any diseased material to make compost from. Either burn it or remove it from your property altogether.

CUTWORMS: COLLAR IT

● If you are troubled by cutworms eating your newly-planted seedlings, rather than using bait try surrounding each little plant with a collar made from the central cardboard core of a toilet roll or the various wrapping papers used in the kitchen, cut to a suitable length. These collars protect the young plants until they are strong enough to withstand later attacks by cutworms.

● An even more effective method is to use small tins, such as those in which tuna or salmon are packaged. Cut both tops and bottoms from the tins and place the resulting cylinders around the seedlings.

RED SPIDER MITES: CHILL THEIR ENTHUSIASM

Spray these pests with iced water and watch them disappear. Keep on doing this as you see them appear and eventually they will move away altogether.

PREVENT PROBLEMS IN THE FIRST PLACE

Many pest and disease problems in the garden can be prevented before they even occur. For example, choose plant varieties which are resistant to pests and diseases; some plants are being bred with just this in mind. If the plants are growing strongly and happily they will not succumb to pest or disease attacks. Make sure you choose the right plants for the situation (bear in mind sun or shade and soil type), and water and feed regularly to make sure they are in tip-top condition. Some problems are caused by poor garden hygiene. Clear up fallen leaves and other garden rubbish and clear away and burn any diseased material you do find to prevent it spreading to other plants. Above all be vigilant – if you catch problems early they will be much easier to deal with.

MOLES: PUT THEM OFF WITH BAD ODOURS

● Place raw onions in mole runs to chase them away. Peeled garlic has the same effect and in fact some mole repellents use this as an active ingredient.

● Plant *Euphorbia lathyrus* in your garden – the roots give off an odour that moles hate.

SLUGS: LURE THEM WITH BEER, KILL THEM IN HOT WATER

● Slugs love beer. Many garden pests have an extremely well-developed sense of smell and a beer-baited trap can be successful in catching slugs and snails. Sink an empty tin can flush with ground level somewhere near young plants or those that are coming out of winter dormancy. Make up a mixture of half a cup of beer, a cup of water and a teaspoon of brown sugar and fill the tin – the pests will be attracted to the smell and fall into the tin and drown. Slugs will eat anything, including each other, and seem to be more difficult to eradicate than snails.

● Place grapefruit skins, cut side down, on the soil around vulnerable plants. The slugs will collect underneath these and can then be collected and destroyed by tossing them into a bucket of very hot saltwater.

● Use fresh sawdust around the base of the plant as a barrier, as slugs are most reluctant to crawl over the wood shavings.

SNAILS: USE HANDY HOUSEHOLD PRODUCTS

● Snails will not crawl across broken egg shells, used coffee grounds, sharp sand or coarse gravel, so place these materials around the plants you are trying to protect. Also try the ash from a wood fire (don't use ash from coal or anthracite fires as it contains harmful chemicals that will kill the plant and be bad for the soil). Wood ash, however, also adds potassium, a trace element needed for healthy plant growth.

● If you have a plant that snails and slugs enjoy eating growing in a container, smear a thick layer of petroleum jelly around the rim of the pot. It is water resistant and the snails will not cross this barrier.

● Use an empty margarine tub filled with beer to attract snails. They will climb inside the tub and drown.

Also see Organic Alternatives and House Plants tips

COARSE GRAVEL

BROKEN EGG SHELLS

SHARP SAND

USED COFFEE GROUNDS

KEEP SUSCEPTIBLE PLANTS SEPARATE

In order to protect certain plants that are susceptible to attack from worms, snails or slugs, consider planting them in containers that can be kept on a patio or somewhere where they will not easily be reached. Plants that would benefit from this include hostas, petunias and agapanthus.

Planting & transplanting

REPLICATE THE SOIL HEIGHT

When planting any plant from a container into the garden, make sure that the soil level around the plant in the container – be this a plastic bag from the nursery or a rigid container such as a plastic pot – is replicated in the garden.

KEEP THE SAME SIDE TO THE SUN

When transplanting a shrub or a tree, always mark the side that is facing north with a piece of coloured string or a dab of paint. When you place the plant in its new position, make sure that it once again faces the same direction. This way it remains in the same sun aspect that it was growing in, ensuring that the same side is exposed to the hot sun – the cells of the plant that are on the sunnier side are different to those on the lee side. A plant that does not have to change its cell structure will adapt more quickly.

TEASE APART THE ROOTS

If the plant you have bought in the nursery shows signs of being slightly rootbound, with masses of tightly growing roots and very little soil showing, gently tease the roots apart before planting. Use your fingers or a garden fork to do this, being extremely careful not to damage the roots in any way. Spread them out before filling in the planting hole with soil.

Plants that are rootbound have lots of roots on the surface of the rootball, often encircling it. However, the presence of lots of fine, white hair roots is an indication that the plant is not rootbound.

PLANT IN AUTUMN FOR BEST RESULTS

Autumn is a wonderful time for planting. Not only are the days cooler, making gardening more pleasant, but plants respond better when planted during this season. Although cooler days cause plants to slow their leaf growth, the leaves continue to produce food that can be used to develop the roots. Also, with the slowing-down process, plants are more easily transplanted as they need less moisture.

If the soil does not freeze over winter, autumn-planted trees and shrubs can develop a large root system in autumn and early spring, and be ready to grow much faster when the warmer weather arrives. A tree or shrub planted in autumn will be almost double the size of one planted in spring, after only two seasons of growth.

USE FILLERS RATHER THAN PLANTING TOO CLOSELY

Plant shrubs and trees at the recommended spacing as indicated on their labels. It might look better to plant them closer together for an immediate effect but within a short space of time the shrubs will have grown up and then you might need to prune heavily or even remove some, thereby wasting money.

Once you have planted your trees and shrubs at the recommended spacing, make use of cheaper 'filler' plants such as fuchsias, hebes or any quick-growing perennial or annual that can be removed as the choice plants grow and need more room. Your nursery should have reasonably priced mixed packs of seeds that simply require scattering and a light raking in. These will give you masses of colour in a short space of time at little cost whilst the other shrubs are busy growing, and will take care of bare and exposed soil.

Also see Seed Sowing tips

FIRST CUT ESTABLISHED PLANTS BACK

If you need to transplant a shrub or tree because it is in the wrong place, do so in early spring. Deciduous plants transplant more easily than evergreens. You may choose to move the entire plant as it is, or you can remove half the number of stems to compensate for the roots that will be lost as the plant is dug out of the soil. Cut these stems off at ground level before digging the plant out.

You may even consider cutting the entire plant back by a third to half of its original size before moving it, to conserve the sap inside the stems. Remember that the plant will be severely stressed and will need a little extra care in the form of sufficient water whilst it is re-establishing itself – but don't overwater at this stage either. Too much water might cause the damaged plant roots to start rotting.

DON'T MIX CLAY WITH LOAM

When planting shrubs and trees in clay soil, make a mound of sharp sand inside the hole to prevent the roots from becoming waterlogged after heavy rain. Never refill a hole in the clay soil with loamy topsoil or compost as the clay soil will simply create a sump in which the roots will drown. Rather refill the hole with the same clay soil that was dug out of it, but mixed with some compost and fertilizer. The resistance that the same clay soil filling will afford to water will prevent the roots from drowning.

GO BIG WITH THE HOLES

The hole for a newly-bought shrub must be at least twice the size of the container that it is growing in. The more organic material in the form of compost and manure you use during the planting process, the more richly rewarded you will be when the plant starts to grow and thrive on all the food you put into the hole. When planting young trees, ensure that the hole is a minimum of 1m (3ft) in length, breadth and depth, with square sides and bottom.

DIG SQUARE HOLES

When you are digging a hole for a tree, or any other plant for that matter, make sure that you dig the hole square. This applies especially to where the sides meet the bottom of the hole. A tree that has been planted in a round-bottomed hole has less chance of getting its roots to penetrate the soil that was left undisturbed. If a root meets a square-sided wall, the pressure in the growing tip of the root will make sure that it penetrates the soil.

Trees planted in round holes could end up with roots growing in circles around the main root ball as they have not been able to penetrate the rounded surfaces inside the hole. This also means that the tree has not sent its roots into the surrounding soil to get the nutrients required and has not been able to anchor itself in the soil, making it more likely to blow over in the wind.

Pruning

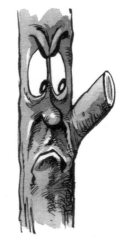

KEEP THE CUT SURFACE FLUSH WITH THE MAIN STEM

When pruning large branches off a tree, make sure that the branch is sawn off flush with the main stem. Do not leave any form of stump behind as this is most unsightly. A flush-cut surface allows the wound to heal faster and disappear, so that in time it will be hard to see that the limb ever existed. The same principle applies when using secateurs – always cut with the flat side of the secateurs against the main limb from which you are removing the branch. This gives you a nice clean flush cut and also does not leave unsightly bumps on the side of the stem.

Also see Fruit Trees tips

TRIM TO RESHAPE

Rather than severe pruning, it's better to trim to reshape hedges and topiary specimens – these plants will only need to be pruned if they ever become too old or too woody.

Also see Hedges tips

MAKE A CLEAN, SHARP CUT

Be sure to make clean cuts when pruning and do not leave ragged pieces, as these will start to decay and will cause damage to the plants' stems. Clean cuts are easily achieved by keeping your pruning tools very sharp at all times.

Also see Tools tips

ERR ON THE SIDE OF CAUTION

The harder you prune a plant, the more vigorous the results usually will be. However, if you are unsure of how much to prune, under- rather than over-prune a plant – you can always prune again the next year or even later in the same year if needs be. If you are really unsure about a plant's needs then do not prune at all. It will be quite happy to be left alone. Some plants dislike pruning so much that they never recover afterwards.

FIRST DECREASE THE WEIGHT

When cutting a heavy branch off, first cut off a section at the end to reduce the weight of the branch. Now cut the remaining stump off flush with the trunk of the tree. This avoids large tears in the bark and prevents infections setting in.

CUT BRANCHES WITH UNDERCUTS AND PRESSURE

When cutting a large branch, first make an undercut at least a third of the way through the branch and then saw from the top. This will ensure that the branch snaps off cleanly at exactly the place you want to remove it.

When cutting thick or hard wood, push the branch that is being cut away from you, but without applying too much pressure. Keep the cutting edge going in the same direction as the branch is being pushed and the cut will be easier to make.

UNDERCUT

CUT OFF DYING PARTS QUICKLY

If any piece of a plant dies, prune it off as quickly as possible, no matter the time of year. In this way you can prevent the die-back from continuing any further – you particularly want to avoid the die-back reaching the main stem of the plant.

MOVE PLANTS RATHER THAN PRUNING TOO OFTEN

If plants are too close together, it might be worth transplanting the offending individual to somewhere in the garden where it has more space to grow. If you move this poor plant, it will not get hacked back every year and will be allowed to grow in peace.

Also see Planting & Transplanting tips

USE SAWN-OFF BRANCHES TO SUPPORT OTHERS

Collect all the sturdy branches that you have pruned and use them in a wigwam shape to support climbers such as sweetpeas and runner beans.

COMPLETELY ERADICATE DISEASED WOOD

Any diseased wood that is pruned from a plant must not be composted. Instead burn it all or take it to a rubbish tip. If you place it on the compost heap, the disease will continue to multiply under these ideal conditions and you will return it to the garden when you dig in the compost at a later stage.

Also see Organic Alternatives tips

GIVE LIFE TO OLD PLANTS BY PRUNING HARD

Rejuvenate old shrubs by pruning or cutting back the entire plant to knee height. (This should only be done when the plant has outgrown its space or has become old and woody.) Also remove the very thin and/or the very old thick stems.

   Be warned however that this drastic method has both risks and advantages. If the shrub is in a poor condition, it might not recover. But, if it does respond well, then you will soon have a beautiful, virtually 'new' plant full of young stems and new growth of flowers or foliage. Spring is the best time to perform this drastic pruning.

DON'T PRUNE DURING A DROUGHT

You must be able to water the plants enough to sustain the newly formed shoots as they begin to grow, so only prune when you are assured of sufficient water to enable you to do so. *Also see Watering tips*

ALLOW CONIFERS ONLY ONE STEM

Upright-growing conifers should have one main stem to maintain their perfect teardrop shape. If a plant develops a second stem, prune out the smaller of the two. Cut it as close to where it emerges from the main stem as possible and as early in its life as possible, before it tries to become dominant.

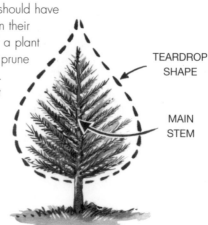

TEARDROP SHAPE

MAIN STEM

PRUNE PLANTS IN SEASON

If you intend pruning trees and shrubs, do so in the winter months when they are resting. As the temperatures start to rise, so the activity inside the plant increases. In winter there will also not be any bird nests with eggs or chicks in them that might be destroyed or harmed in the process.

As a very general rule of thumb:

- **Prune deciduous shrubs** as they go out of bloom.
- **Prune evergreen shrubs** as they start active growth.
- **Prune summer-flowering shrubs** just before growth begins in spring.
- **Prune spring-flowering shrubs** immediately after flowering.
- **Prune deciduous trees** in early spring, but wait until maples and birch trees are in full leaf before pruning to reduce 'bleeding'.

PRUNE A ROSE QUICKLY AND SIMPLY

The fastest way to prune a rose is to select the three of four stems that you intend keeping, cut these off at the correct height (which depends on the variety of rose) and then just cut away everything else that is on the plant. Select the best, young green stems grown during that year to keep and remove all the dark, thick, old stems.

Also see Rose tips

BEWARE OF PLANTS WITH MILKY SAP

Consider any plant that exudes a white milky substance when cut as extremely dangerous, especially oleanders and euphorbias. Some can cause blindness if their milk gets into your eyes.

USE SUITABLE PROTECTIVE CLOTHING

If you have an old pair of long boots or gum boots, cut off the leg pieces and use them to cover your arms to prevent thorns or sharp pieces of wood tearing and damaging your skin while you prune. Some plants have poison in their thorns or leaves, so make sure you are well covered to prevent any tears or scratches leading to nasty infected skin wounds.

ROSES

BUY DISEASE-RESISTANT VARIETIES

To do away with the problems traditionally associated with growing roses, such as mildew and black spot, use varieties that are more resistant to pests and diseases. Good examples are the old-fashioned David Austin English roses as well as the Flower Carpet series, which show remarkable resistance to disease and flower very freely. The majority are also highly scented, have a varied range of colours, need little attention and don't necessarily have to be pruned each year to give a magnificent display of flowers.

DON'T RISK TOO LITTLE SUN

Roses really do prefer to be grown in a position that provides them with sun all day long. You can get away with a minimum of six hours of sun in summer for varieties such as Iceberg, which can be planted where they'll get full morning sun and light shade in the afternoon. This will depend on the exact aspect in your garden and will be a matter of trial and error, so avoid costly mistakes by simply keeping them in full sun. Roses that do not get enough sun are prone to developing long, thin branches that easily break off or droop, as well as being very susceptible to diseases on the leaves, such as mildew and black spot.

SUMMER-PRUNE FOR A SECOND FLUSH

After the first flush of flowers, all roses should be cut back by a third of their original size. This will give you a second flush of flowers similar to the one in spring, and your entire rose garden will be in flower.

NEVER CULTIVATE ROSE BEDS TOO DEEPLY

Roses hate having their fine surface roots disturbed – these roots are the ones responsible for the absorption of nutrients from the soil and are therefore very important to the future well-being of the plant.

MULCHING ROSE BEDS

Bark chips and cocoa shell make excellent mulches for use in the rose garden as they do not break down too quickly and also look attractive. Both are available in sacks from garden centres, but you could buy them cheaper if you order them loose from a wholesaler. Mulching the beds will keep the soil moist and cut down on weeding.

Also see Mulching tips

USE COMPANION PLANTS TO ELIMINATE PESTS

Garlic, basil and scented pelargoniums are good companion plants for the rose garden as they will keep aphids and beetles to a minimum by giving off scents and aromas that are disliked by these pests.

Also see Pests & Diseases and Organic Alternatives tips

CHOOSE LOW-GROWING SUN-LOVERS AS GROUNDCOVERS

Many types of plants are excellent for use in the rose garden as groundcover for the bare soil around the plants. Examples include alyssum (which can be bought in seed form and scattered, followed just by gentle raking into the soil and watering), *Ajuga reptans*, silver-leaved lambs' ears, cat mint, thyme, parsley, Virginia stocks – in fact almost any low-growing plants which like sunny conditions.

GO EASY ON THE PICKING EARLY IN THE SEASON

Don't cut too many stems with blooms from the same plant all at once, especially early in the spring when the plant has just produced its new growth after being pruned. Remember that the plant has to have leaves to produce new stems and flowers, so give it all the help you can by keeping as many leaves on the plant as possible at all times. Only pick long stems if you need them for the vase, otherwise keep the stems you pick as short as possible. Later in the season when the plant has grown well and is full of new stems and leaves you can pick those longer ones without robbing the plant of too many leaves.

SNAP OFF DEAD FLOWERS

Rather than cutting back the entire stem once it has produced blooms, snap off the dead flower at its base, thereby also removing the ovary where the seeds are forming. Simply hold the dead flower in the palm of your hand and place two fingers under the thickened part where the flower meets the stem – this is the ovary. With a quick snap of your wrist, the flower will break off easily, leaving most of the stem and leaves with which the bush can produce more flowers. The plant will form new shoots from wherever it feels necessary.

GROW PARSLEY NEAR ROSES

Use parsley as a groundcover in your rose garden as it increases the fragrance in the blooms.
Also see Groundcover tips

PLAN THE TIMING OF THAT SPECTACULAR DISPLAY

If your garden is going to be used for a function other than in early summer when the first flush of flowers has appeared after pruning, and you need a spectacular show of flowers, prune the rose bushes back to half their size eight weeks prior to the day of the function. Apply special rose fertilizer to the roots and keep the plants well watered. Use this method any time through spring and summer to ensure all the roses are in full bloom on the day you will need them. Later than this, however, and autumn will have set in and the plants will not respond as well.

NIP OUT THE CENTRAL BUD ON CLUSTER-FLOWERED ROSES

As the heads on cluster-flowered roses start to develop, remove the largest central bud from the cluster before it opens. (Cluster-flowered are the roses that produce large masses of flowers at the ends of the stems.) Removal of the central bud ensures that the rest of the blooms on the stem open simultaneously, thereby maximizing their effect. The central bud is the first flower to open if left on the plant.

PUT A HEDGE CLIPPER TO MINIATURES

To prune miniature roses, simply take a hedge clipper and cut them back to a third (or even half, if they have grown very well) of their original size. Remove any dead stems and thin out the remaining branches to avoid the plant becoming overcrowded – you want to end up with an evenly-branched plant.

THROW OUT THE TEXTBOOK AND JUST CUT BACK

If you don't have the interest or the knowledge to prune correctly, simply cut back the entire plant to half its original size in early spring. Cut it all off at one level, then remove the dead stems and some of the old thick ones. If there are any stems that cross the plant, remove these as well (this is purely for aesthetic reasons, and so is not a must). Leave the rest to nature and the plant will shoot out and flower for you. In fact, you might even find that the plant pruned in this way gives you more flowers than those pruned strictly according to textbook rules.

Also see Pruning tips

CUT STEMS AT AN ANGLE

Prune rose stems at a 45° angle 5mm (1/4in) above an outward-pointing bud. This will encourage the new shoot to grow towards the outside of the plant and keep the centre of the plant open to allow sunlight to get into the middle of the bush.

SEED SOWING

MIX FINE SEEDS WITH SHARP SAND

When sowing extremely fine seeds, mix them with something that is easy to see on the surface of the compost as you sprinkle the seeds. In this way you can tell where the mixture you are sprinkling has landed and you won't sow too many seeds in one place in the tray and so cause overcrowding of the plants.

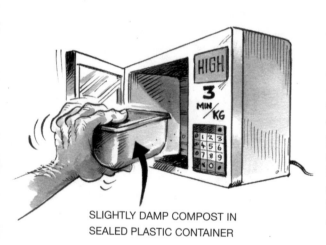

SLIGHTLY DAMP COMPOST IN
SEALED PLASTIC CONTAINER

STERILIZE COMPOST IN YOUR MICROWAVE

If you are using small quantities of compost to sow your seeds in, simply microwave it to kill off any disease-causing pathogens or weed seeds that might be present. Make sure that the compost is slightly damp; place it in a sealed plastic container and microwave on high for three minutes per 1kg (2lb).
Also see Weeds tips

BATHE RATHER THAN SPRAY FRESH SEED TRAYS

Stand the tray of sown seeds in a shallow dish of water and allow the water to rise to the surface of the compost. As you see the top of the compost becoming moist, remove the tray immediately to prevent the seeds from floating up to the surface. This method of watering will prevent the seeds being washed into the corners. You can also use a watering can that has a very fine nozzle, but be extremely careful not to cause the compost to wash to one side, taking all the freshly sewn seed with it.
Also see Watering tips

SAVE MONEY BY RECYCLING

● Square plastic supermarket boxes, used to package strawberries and other fruits, make excellent seed-sowing containers. Remember to wash thoroughly and to ensure good drainage by making holes in the bases.

● Circular cardboard tubes, egg trays and plastic yoghurt, cottage cheese or cream containers make perfect seed trays for sowing individual seeds of things like sweetpeas and cucumbers. Just be sure to pierce holes in the bottom of the plastic containers for drainage.

DON'T SOW TOO MANY SEEDS AT ONCE

Only sow what you are going to need. It's pointless sowing more than you can use and wasting the leftovers. (Unless of course you plan to give them away to the neighbours or trade with other eager seed sowers.) This is especially true of vegetable seeds – do you really need 100 cabbages? Instead, sow five seeds each week if that is what you estimate your consumption will be, or even sow seven and transplant only the five strongest into the vegetable plot.

Also see Vegetables tips

SOW SEEDS ON A WIND-FREE, DRY DAY

You don't want your precious seeds blowing away or ending up outside the furrows that were so carefully made for them.

COVER ALL SEED BEDS AFTER SOWING

Beware of heavy rain or even a wrongly directed hosepipe, which can both wash away fine seeds or cover them too deeply in soil. If you have just sown seeds and rain looks imminent, cover the entire area with plastic sheeting or hessian. A sheet of glass placed over the seed trays works excellently, but ensure good ventilation by placing a short stick in each corner of the tray to lift the glass away from the surface of the compost. Don't forget to remove the sheeting as soon as the rain is over.

Clear plastic sheeting can also be used to create a miniature hothouse for your seed trays. Simply take a few green branches, bend them in a hoop well above the height of the compost in the tray and drape the plastic over this frame. Leave spaces at the bottom near the compost level for circulation and to allow air to escape.

WAIT FOR THE FIRST TRUE LEAVES BEFORE TRANSPLANTING

The very first couple of leaves that are produced by the seed will be single leaves. When two leaves emerge opposite each other (usually larger and sometimes even a different shape to the first ones produced), these can be considered the first true leaves. Now you can transplant into seed trays, keeping the seedlings well spaced in neat lines to allow each plant to receive the maximum amount of light and develop fully. Once the seedlings are covered in leaves and well established, they can be transplanted into the garden.

Whilst seedlings are still in their trays, a very weak solution of liquid fertilizer can be applied weekly to encourage rapid growth. Make sure that the compost in the container is kept moist at all times.

STORE SEED IN AIRTIGHT CONTAINERS

Empty plastic camera film containers are a great storage option for leftover or collected seed. Label each one individually – in fact, make double-sure by writing the name of the seed on a small piece of paper and placing this inside the container.

Alternatively, store seed packets in a glass jar with a tight-fitting lid and place a sachet of desiccant or a tablespoon of powdered milk in the jar with the seed packets to keep them dry. Seal the jar and keep it in the fridge – but never the freezer.

DON'T ALLOW SEEDLINGS IN TRAYS TO FLOWER

Remove any flowers that appear on the seedlings whilst they are still in their trays. The idea is to maximize the young plants' growth potential. They should be allowed to flower only once they are well established in the garden.

TEST THE VIABILITY OF OLD SEED

Put 10–12 seeds between sheets of damp paper towel and seal this in a plastic food storage bag or container in a warm place away from direct sun. Every few days check to see whether the seeds have sprouted and that the paper is still damp. If more than half of the seeds sprout, you have an indication that the packet of seed is still good enough to use. If you are testing several packets, be sure to accurately label the storage containers with the names of each seed type.

SELECTING PLANTS

BUY FLOWERING TREES AND SHRUBS WHEN IN FLOWER

If you can wait, buy flowering trees, shrubs, groundcover and perennials when they are in flower in the nursery to make absolutely sure that the colour of the flower fits in with your colour scheme. Just because the label on the plant says 'cerise', there is absolutely no guarantee that this is the colour cerise that you had in mind. On the other hand, don't be tempted by those magnificent flowering specimens. As difficult as it may be, try to resist buying plants on impulse just because they look beautiful and are in full flower. Carefully consider whether you have the right spot for the plant in question, and whether it will fit in with the overall design of the area you want to plant it in.

SELECT HEALTHY PLANTS

Do not buy a plant that has any of the following danger signs: yellowing or wilted leaves, a broken container, roots growing through the bottom of the container, or any stem that is diseased or malformed. Also, never buy a plant that is rootbound. Sometimes nurseries cut back plants that have become too big for their containers to try to rejuvenate them. Rather select a young, sometimes smaller specimen that has healthy young leaves and is growing well.

BEWARE THE BIG SPECIMENS

A large well-established plant is not always the best buy, so don't necessarily buy the biggest size you can afford. Some of these plants have been in their containers for many years and may already be stunted. Often the results are better if you look for a younger, vigorous, healthy-growing specimen that, once planted, will likely overtake the one that has been in its container so long. The younger plant has never had a setback and is ready to grow.

Also see Container Gardening tips

Shrubs

ENSURE GOOD AIR CIRCULATION

If you live in a cool, moist and misty area, space your shrubs further apart than usually recommended. This helps to allow more air movement through the plants and will help to prevent fungal spores being trapped within the plants, causing mildew and fungal diseases.

PLANT CONTRASTING FOLIAGE SHRUBS TOGETHER

To increase the perceived intensity of colours, plant shrubs selected for autumn foliage colour next to, or in front of, other plants that have evergreen or silvery-grey foliage.

GROW YOUR OWN STANDARD

It is easy to make standards of most shrubs with a suckering habit. Dig out a sucker with a decent bit of root attached. Strip off the lower leaves and branches, leaving a neat 'top-knot'. Plant in a pot that is in proportion to the size of the piece that you have dug up and after a few weeks, when new growth starts, pinch out the growing tips of the branches forming the top-knot to encourage bushy growth. Discourage any further suckering of the potted standard and keep the stem clean by brushing off any unwanted buds and shoots that emerge – simply rub them hard with your fingers.

To grow any shrub into a standard, you must select a plant that has a single main stem with an intact growing tip. Don't let side shoots develop, but allow the plant to grow to the desired height and then nip out the growing tip. The plant will soon start to develop side branches at the top – these will form the main framework of the round ball at the top of the standard. Keep on pinching out the growing tips on all the branches to encourage them all to branch even more, thereby creating a very well branched and full 'head' on your standard.

STAKING

RECYCLE OLD TIGHTS

Unwanted ladies' stockings and tights make excellent ties for use in staking and tying up plants. The material used in the manufacture of stockings is very long lasting, will not rot and is soft enough not to damage the bark of the plant.

DON'T MAKE TIES TOO TIGHT

When staking plants, remember that the plant is in the process of growing and thickening its stems all the time. To prevent the ties biting into the developing stems, allow enough room for a year's growth. This also prevents you having to check on your ties every few months.

TIE PLANTS WITH A FIGURE-OF-EIGHT

Always make the tie between the stem of the plant and the pole you are using for the stake in the form of a figure-of-eight. This allows for expansion and prevents the stem rubbing against the pole if there is any wind.

FORCE THE PLANT TO STRENGTHEN ITS STEM AS QUICKLY AS POSSIBLE

Don't tie plant stakes too high up the tree – tying them about a third of the way up gives the tree enough support to prevent it falling over or breaking off in a strong wind. Making the tie lower than usual encourages the tree to harden its stem more quickly and so ensures it can support itself better, rather than just relying on the stake. A stake that is angled low, like a tent-peg, will allow the tree's top to flex in the wind, forcing the trunk to strengthen. Top-grafted standards, such as weeping trees, are the exception – they need to have a stake that reaches to just below the graft point. Loosen the tie as the trunk expands.

COVER WIRE TO PREVENT IT DAMAGING THE STEM

Use a piece of old hosepipe to cover the wire used in staking – cut a piece long enough to go around the stem of the plant with some extra room for expansion. Make slits in the hosepipe almost all the way through and at regular intervals. Thread the wire through the hosepipe and then bend it to form a circle around the stem of the plant. With a couple of twists in the wire, close the hosepipe ring and then tie it securely to the pole. Now the wire will be prevented from cutting through the plant stem at any stage.

HAMMER THE STAKE IN FIRST

When planting trees, remember always to hammer the stake securely into the ground after you have dug the hole and before you plant the tree. This ensures that the pole is inserted into hard, undisturbed soil and is therefore more secure. It also prevents your accidentally pushing the stake through the root ball of the tree and damaging the roots.

Also see Planting & Transplanting tips

STEPS

FAVOUR ROUGH TEXTURES

When constructing steps in a shady part of the garden, be sure that they have a rough finish – a shady situation encourages the growth of moss and algae which makes steps dangerously slippery. Bricks are probably best – not only are they rough but they're small enough to ensure your foot doesn't slip too far before being stopped by the gaps in between. Steps built with natural stones are less likely to be slippery because of their unevenness and rough texture.

CLEAN STEPS WITH CHANGES IN PH

If steps have become dangerously slippery with moss or algae, they can be cleaned with a weak solution of swimming pool chlorine: dissolve one cup of powder in 5 litres (9 pints) of water and sprinkle this over the steps. Be very careful not to get the mixture onto plants as it will burn their roots and kill them. To kill off moss that is growing on steps, wet the area thoroughly and then sprinkle liberally with agricultural lime. The high alkalinity of the lime will quickly get rid of the acid-loving moss.

Tools

BUY LAWNMOWERS WISELY

There is no such thing as the best type of lawnmower – rather look for the one that best suits your own needs. The bigger the lawn, the bigger the machine should be to mow the area as quickly as possible – whether to buy a petrol or electric machine is up to you. However remember that hand-pushed mowers are only for those that need the exercise or have a very small lawn. As tempting as it might be, do not buy a ride-on mower to cut a small lawn as it will make mowing more, rather than less, time-consuming – the large turning area needed by ride-on mowers makes them difficult to manage.

Also see Lawns tips

DON'T FORGET THE SAFETY BASICS

Owners of power mowers, ride-on mowers and in particular rotary mowers should cover their legs when they operate their machines. Jeans are fine, but shorts are definitely not recommended. Avoid loose-fitting clothes that can get caught in the moving parts. Always wear shoes to protect your feet from the mower blades – open sandals are really not suitable. Keep feet away from the body of the machine – in other words, don't walk into it. Never leave a running motor unattended.

DON'T BRUISE THE PLANT WITH BLUNT INSTRUMENTS

Instead of a clean cut, blunt secateurs can bruise the plant and in turn allow disease and infection to set in.

Also see Fruit Trees tips

MAKE YOURSELF A HOLSTER

Cut slits in the side of an old spectacle case and slip a belt through them. Use the case as a holster for secateurs.

WEIGHT THE FRONT OF THE WHEELBARROW

When loading a wheelbarrow, always try to keep the most weight over the wheel section – this makes for easier handling and less strain on your back.

CHOOSE WOODEN HANDLES FOR COMFORT, METAL FOR DURABILITY

Wooden-handled tools are warmer to work with in winter than metal ones. These handles are usually easier to replace than metal ones, with spares more easily found. However, metal handles are stronger and more durable, though they get very hot if left in the sun for any length of time, so don't forget to place them in the shade when you're not using them.

OVERTURN WHEELBARROWS

By keeping them overturned when not in use, you will prevent water collecting inside them and forming rust.

KEEP TOOLS SHARP

Sharp cutting edges on digging tools penetrate the soil more easily. The easiest way of sharpening tools is with a metal hand file – buy the largest one you can find, as one or two strokes of the file will sharpen the entire edge. If the cutting edge of the tool becomes too blunt, take it to your lawnmower shop and ask them to sharpen it on an electric grinding stone. Make sure that all cutting edges of secateurs, pruners or saws are also kept sharp and free of rust. The sharper the cutting edge, the easier it is to cut with the instrument and the thicker the branch you will be able to manage easily.

Also see Fruit Trees and Pruning tips

PAINT THE TOOL RED

To avoid losing tools such as trowels and weeders among plants, paint their handles a bright colour that can easily be seen from anywhere. Red and yellow are usually the best options.

MOISTEN SOIL BEFORE DIGGING

Always try to water dry soil before digging as this will make the task much easier – moist soil is softer than dry soil.

Also see Watering tips

CONVERT YOUR OWN TOOLS

Long-handled tools are easy to make: simply remove the short handles of hand tools and replace with wooden broomstick handles.

TREES

USE A PENCIL TO MEASURE THE HEIGHT OF A TREE

Stand well back from the tree. Hold a pencil at arm's length in your line of sight and align it exactly, top and bottom, with the top and bottom of the tree by moving backwards or forwards. Then, without moving from where you're now standing, turn the pencil sideways and hold it parallel to the ground, keeping the bottom of the pencil in line with your vision of the base of the tree. Mentally mark where the top of the pencil appears to meet the ground, then measure the distance from the actual tree trunk to this point on the ground. This will be the height of the tree.

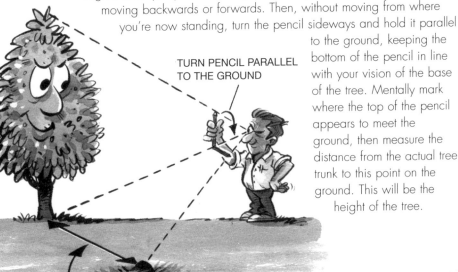

TURN PENCIL PARALLEL TO THE GROUND

HEIGHT OF TREE

FEED AND WATER ALONG THE DRIP LINE

Trees absorb most of their nutrients at the drip line of the leaves – that area on the ground in line with the widest reach of the canopy, where the branches and leaves end. When fertilizing or even watering trees, concentrate on placing the fertilizer in this area even if there are other plants beneath the tree.

A good idea is to spike this area well with a fork beforehand. You can also make large, deep holes using a pronged instrument such as a sharpened steel rod. Pour the fertilizer down these holes and then cover with loose soil. As you apply water, or when it rains, the fertilizer will dissolve and be available in the area where most of the roots are. This is also a good method when applying fungicides to trees that are affected by disease, such as powdery mildew on oaks or planes.

Also see Feeding and Watering tips

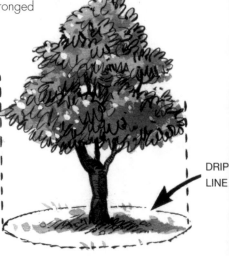

DRIP LINE

KEEP AN EYE ON DEAD TREES

That dead tree you tried to disguise with a creeper could fall over after heavy rains. This is especially true if the tree has been dead for a number of years and the wood has started to decay or ants have chosen to make it their home. Be especially wary of the damage that can be caused by dead trees falling near the house.

USE TREES TO REGULATE TEMPERATURE

Plant trees close to your house if you live in an exposed place. The leaves will shade the house and keep it cool, acting as an air-conditioner on hot summer days. Choose a deciduous tree that will lose its leaves in winter, thereby allowing the warm rays of the sun to enter and warm the house during the cold months.

PREVENT HOLES IN
TREES FROM ROTTING

If a limb from a tree has been lost and the wound has not healed properly, you might find that the tree has started rotting and a large cavity or hole has formed. To prevent this going any further you must scrape out the inside of the cavity until you reach clean, fresh living wood. Use a wound sealer to cover the exposed fresh wood and fill the cavity with a concrete mixture, ensuring that the edges are exactly in line with the bark of the tree. You will find that after a time the bark will start to grow over the concrete and eventually close the wound altogether, thus saving the tree from deteriorating any further.

PROTECT THE BARK OF TREES
GROWING IN THE LAWN

When planting a tree in a lawn always leave a bare area around the stem to prevent the bark of the tree from being hit by the lawnmower or cut and damaged by the blades of a strimmer or edging machine. Once the tree has had its bark cut off, known as ring-barking, it will probably die.

Where grass has been allowed to grow right up against the stem, use hard-wearing material such as rubber from an inner tube to wrap around the stem while mowing.
Also see Lawns tips

LEAVE NESTING SITES
IN HOLES IN TREES

Small cavities in trees are great nesting sites for birds. Unless the hole is getting bigger and rotting, leave it alone and it will heal itself naturally over time. In the meantime birds will use these holes for nesting in without damaging the tree.

RING-BARK
UNWANTED TREES

To get rid of a tree without using chemicals, simply cut around the base of its stem and remove a ring of at least 10cm (4in) of bark. The tree will slowly die. Be absolutely sure that the tree is really not needed – it takes a long time to grow and is very easily killed. The old adage 'think twice, cut once' is very wise, so make completely certain you are not going to regret your decision.

VEGETABLES

SHADE LEAF CROPS

To ensure success with salad crops such as lettuce, plant them where they will receive afternoon shade. Salad leaf crops definitely prefer being out of the hot afternoon sun – even better would be to plant them under shade cloth cover.

KEEP VEGETABLE BEDS NARROW

Use long, narrow beds instead of wide ones to make it easier to reach the plants.

PLANT IN NORTH/SOUTH ROWS

Planting in this way will ensure that all your plants get an equal amount of sunlight on all sides.

WATER ACCURATELY

All vegetables need at least 2.5cm (1in) of water per week – this converts to about 25 litres (40 pints) per square metre (yard) per week. The simplest way to measure rainfall or overhead irrigation is with a rain gauge installed in the vegetable plot. Surface watering is best gauged by inspecting the soil. The correct amount of water will penetrate clay soils to a depth of around 10–15cm (4–6in). Sandy soils will be wet to a greater depth, but will also drain so rapidly that it is wiser to apply half the amount of water twice a week.

Vegetables must never go short of water. Root crops such as carrots will split when watered sporadically. Leafy crops such as lettuce and cabbage yield good crops if watered regularly, and vegetables such as peas and beans will produce more pods if water is plentiful at flowering time. Tomatoes and squash also benefit from increased water at flowering time because root activity is reduced.

Also see Watering tips

COVER THE VEGETABLE PLOT WITH SHADE CLOTH

Erect a netted cage over your vegetable garden to protect it from birds and beetles. Fine shade cloth keeps beetles out while allowing all but the most intense sunlight through. Very high temperatures often cause tomatoes, peppers and beans to abort flowers. If this does occur, don't give up on the plants; just keep them well watered and they will produce flowers again when the cooler weather returns.

HANG TOMATOES

Grow the small bunching tomatoes like the 'cherry' types in hanging baskets where they look attractive and are easy to pick. Fruit that is kept off the ground will be cleaner, and the improved air circulation will ensure that it is also healthier. Large tomatoes are obviously too heavy to grow in this way.

KEEP TALLER VARIETIES ON THE SOUTHERN SIDE

Plant tall-growing plants such as sweet-corn on the south side of the vegetable patch so that they do not cast a shadow over the other smaller sun-loving plants.

SOW LESS, MORE OFTEN

Sow fewer seeds at a time, in short rows, and at very regular intervals to ensure the maximum number of vegetables produced get used and that there isn't a glut of the same vegetable at any one time.

Also see Seed Sowing tips

LET THEM CHILL

Some vegetables like getting cold. For fuller, sweeter flavour wait to pick kale, cauliflower, cabbage and carrots until after the first frost has occurred. You will taste the difference.

PRACTISE CROP ROTATION

Avoid always growing the same crop in the same space each year – if there is any form of soil-borne disease that affects one crop, it should die out when a new variety of vegetable is planted.

GO ORGANIC

It really makes good sense to keep the vegetable garden totally organic, using only home-made compost and organic fertilizers in the form of well-rotted manure and seaweed derivatives. (Obviously, home-made compost is guaranteed to be organic because you know what went into it. If you are going to buy compost, make sure that it comes from a reliable organic producer.) Apart from all the health and environmental benefits of going organic, there will be no waiting period before you can eat the vegetable as there might have been had you used a chemical insecticide, and you will find that the vegetables produced in this way are much tastier than when chemicals have been applied to the soil.

Also see Organic Alternatives tips

CHECK FOR WAITING PERIODS

If you are not going the organic route and need to use chemical insecticides on crops in the vegetable garden, be absolutely sure to read the label on the bottle very carefully. Certain chemicals need a window period of up to three weeks before the treated plants are fit to be used for human consumption.

Also see Pesticides & Poisons tips

ATTRACT INSECTS
WITH SCENTED PLANTS

Grow highly scented plants such as jasmine and stocks amongst the vegetables – this will encourage more insects to visit the vegetable garden and help pollinate vegetable plants, giving you better yields.

MIX VEGETABLES IN THE GARDEN
FOR COLOUR AND TEXTURE

If you don't have the space for a dedicated vegetable garden then grow your edibles in amongst your other plants in the garden, where you can create the most wonderful effects. Imagine some beautiful red cabbages planted next to a group of red roses, or red cabbages planted next to a silver-leaved plant such as a globe artichoke. You can create a fantastic colour and texture effect in the garden just by combining the correct vegetable plant with a suitable flowering or foliage plant. In fact you might have so much colour that you may not even need to plant annuals to give added colour to the garden. Vegetables also make excellent companion plants. A group of basil plants will keep aphids away from roses; onions planted next to tomatoes will also act as an insect repellent.

There are many specialized books on companion planting that will tell you all you need to know on the subject.

SAVE MONEY BY
GROWING FROM SEED

Remember that sowing your own vegetable seeds is a cheaper alternative to buying trays of plants from a nursery. They are also guaranteed to be chemical-free from day one. If you are going to buy your seedlings, look out for trays of mixed vegetable plants that will save you planting too many of the same variety.

BEWARE OF CROSS-
POLLINATION

Do not plant hot chilli peppers near green peppers (also known as sweet peppers). The two varieties will cross-pollinate and next year you could end up with very strong green peppers that might be too hot to use raw in salads.

ADD NITROGEN WITH GREEN MANURING

All of the legume family of plants, for example peas, beans and lupins, store nitrogen in their root systems. Once the crop has finished, don't pull the plant out but rather dig it into the soil in the vegetable patch to return the nitrogen to the soil. This is referred to as green manuring.

FEED THE BIRDS AND CATERPILLARS

If you have problems with birds and caterpillars eating your crop, put in some extra plants for them to eat. You will always have enough to share. Especially if you're going organic, plant extra for the worms and caterpillars that might eat the leafy crops.

WATER FEATURES

DON'T FORGET THE FISH

In cold weather remember that the warmest part of the pond is near the bottom, with the temperatures seldom becoming cold enough to kill hardy fish. Problems are more likely to occur if the surface of the pond freezes over, preventing waste gases escaping and oxygen entering the water.

Prevent the freeze-over by floating a ball on the surface of the water, which will ensure that a small area remains ice-free in frosty weather. Alternatives are wooden planks or pieces of polystyrene. If the pond does freeze over, do not be tempted to smash the ice. The shock waves produced can stun or even kill fish. Instead, simply melt a hole in the ice by standing a metal container of hot water on it.

Another winter hazard is overfeeding the fish. They should be able to find enough natural food – if you continue to feed them they may not take it and the uneaten food will contaminate the water. Remember that pond life slows down as the temperature falls.

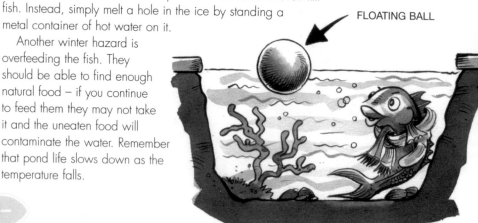

FLOATING BALL

CLARIFY WATER WITH BARLEY WHEAT

If you have a problem with green water in your fish pond or water feature, use barley wheat straw placed in open-weave plastic sacks that are then submerged in the pond. Within about three weeks the decomposing barley straw produces an enzyme that kills off all the green algae in the water and leaves your water crystal clear. Note that other forms of straw such as oat straw do work but not nearly as efficiently as the barley wheat straw.

WATERING

RECYCLE YOUR WATER

Water that has been used in the home for bathing, washing or showering is called grey water and can be used in the garden with certain provisions:

- Soap tends to be on the alkaline side so do not use soapy bath water on things like azaleas, camellias and hydrangeas as they prefer acid soils.
- Trees, shrubs and fruit trees can easily handle bath water.
- In drought conditions use all bath water for anything in order to keep plants alive.
- Never use water from a washing machine, dishwasher or from the kitchen sink that contains detergents that are harmful to plants.
- Similarly never use dirty dishwater – it may contain grease particles, which not only clog the air pockets in the soil but may become smelly as they decompose.
- Avoid using swimming pool water in the garden. Plant roots hate chlorine – it could well kill them. If you have the option of storing the swimming pool water until all the chlorine has evaporated, which usually happens within a couple of days, then by all means do so. Once the chlorine has evaporated the water will be suitable for use.

CHANNEL NATURAL WATER

Consider forming contours as part of your garden landscape to catch and hold water and to prevent water from running away into a street or drain. You can even create small furrows that lead off into the garden beds and redirect the flow of water, so as not to waste it by letting it run away into the street or into a drain.

WATER WHEN IT'S COOL

Watering in summer is best done as soon as the day cools down in the late afternoon or early evening to prevent evaporation and give the water enough time to soak deep into the soil. Water roses early in the morning to avoid them becoming susceptible to fungal disease – the leaves will dry more quickly than they would have if watered later in the day.

Also see Roses tips

WATER LESS BUT MORE THOROUGHLY

Saturate the soil in the area that you are watering before moving on to the next spot. This not only saves water but also forces the plants to develop deep root systems, which in turn makes them less susceptible to drying out or falling over.

INCLUDE A SHUT-OFF FOR RAINY DAYS

When investing in an automatic watering system, ask your installer to include a rain shut-off device so that when you are not at home and it's pouring with rain your irrigation is switched off and does not waste water. These automatic shut-off devices are easily installed and fairly inexpensive and save so much water from being wasted.

SAVE WATER BY DRIP IRRIGATION

A 'drip type' irrigation system, which can be installed by an irrigation expert or by a handyman, uses far less water than the conventional overhead type and gets water right where you need it – at the plant roots. Drip systems are normally installed in the beds where the plants are growing. Small nozzles are inserted into the pipe at regular intervals and the water drips out straight into the soil. In windy areas these systems are also most effective as there is no drift of fine mist spray. Drip systems also ensure that there is less evaporation than with the conventional overhead systems which water an entire surface area.

SAVE THE WATER FOR SPECIAL PLANTS DURING A DROUGHT

In dry weather conditions, save the water you do have for annuals or newly-planted shrubs and trees rather than trying to keep your beautiful green lawn going or to keep well-established shrubs and trees alive. These are better able to withstand drought than the newly-planted ones.

GO FOR LARGE DROPLETS

Sprinklers that produce larger water droplets and need low water pressure are more efficient than those that produce a fine mist-like spray. The added bonus is that coarse droplets of water will not blow away as easily in the wind. Beware of watering plants in the full sun on hot days – the droplets that accumulate on the leaves can act as a powerful magnifying glass and cause scorched blotches on the leaves.

WATER EFFICIENTLY

If you have a water meter or are trying to conserve water in a drought, it is vital that the limited amount of water be used to best advantage.

● On sloping ground

If the garden is on a slope and you wish to water a shrub or tree, water on the higher side just above where the plant is growing. The water will then flow down the slope to the roots on the lower side as well as into the soil on the higher side. It might be a good idea to form a half basin around the lower side of the plant to help to dam the water and prevent it running away too quickly.

● Wet the leaves

Even if you only water precious plants, such as roses, for a short time it will help to give the leaves a quick sprinkling. The idea is to supplement the amount of water the roots can absorb with the extra water absorbed through the leaves, in a process similar to that of foliar feeding. Leaves easily absorb water through their surfaces.

DEEP-SOAK AFTER TRANSPLANTING

When you transplant any plant from the garden, you will always find that the root system you have dug out is very irregular. Once the plant is in its new hole, fill in with soil to about halfway up the roots, then fill the rest of the hole with water, even pushing the hosepipe in and around the roots. This will remove all of the air pockets around the root system and flush the soil into every little crevice. Once the water has drained from the hole, fill it up with soil and make a basin around the top. This basin can once again be filled with water, which should be left to soak away. If the soil level drops too much, top up with more soil to get it to the correct level.
Also see Planting & Transplanting tips

SELECT DROUGHT-TOLERANT SPECIES

If your garden has a dry or rocky area that is difficult to water, plant Mediterranean, drought-tolerant plants or those with fleshy foliage or silver leaves. These are all less likely to suffer under these conditions.
Also see Selecting Plants tips

READ THE WILTING LEAVES

During dry weather conditions, water plants as they begin to show signs of stress, such as wilting leaves. Once the leaves are badly wilted it is more difficult for them to recover. However, don't always assume that wilting or drooping leaves mean that the plant is dry. Check the soil around the plant first before watering – if the roots are damp, it could be that the air temperature is too high, in which case no amount of extra water is going to help. Consider whether the plant is in the wrong place – perhaps it might fare better in a more shady, cooler location in the garden. A quick shower with a fine mist spray might help though.

Plants that have been overwatered because of a lack of good drainage in the soil will show the same wilting symptoms as dry plants do. The overwatered plants' roots will begin to rot and therefore cannot absorb water, leading to a lack of enough water in the plants themselves.

MAKE A SPONGE OF SHREDDED NEWSPAPER

To retain moisture in light, sandy soil, put a layer of shredded newspaper in the bottom of the trenches prepared for planting beans and sweetpeas. The paper will absorb and hold water over a period of time in the bottom of the trench and act like a sponge, releasing the water slowly. It is not wise to use this method of preparation in clay soil, as it might cause the soil to remain too wet for too long.

SHREDDED NEWSPAPER

MULCH MUCH MORE

A thick layer of any form of mulch will decrease the plants' water needs by up to fifty percent. The mulch layer not only serves to trap moisture in the ground but also helps to keep the roots cool and reduce weeds.
Also see Mulching tips

WATER THE SOIL BEFORE PLANTING

Make sure that the ground is well watered before you plant anything. Also make sure that the plant is wet in the container that you bought it in before you remove it. After planting give it a good and thorough soaking.

MAKE A BASIN AROUND NEW PLANTINGS

When you have planted a new plant, form a basin around it to ensure that its roots get an extra soaking while the plant establishes itself.
Also see Planting & Transplanting and Trees tips

TURN DOWN THE PRESSURE

Do not use a high-pressure spray with a fine nozzle on young plants, especially seedlings. The pressure of the water will bruise their leaves.

GROUP PLANTS WITH SIMILAR WATER NEEDS

For example, don't plant succulents in an area where you have plants that need regular watering – the succulents will be overwatered and will rot. The same goes for any plants that prefer dry conditions.

USE OLD HOSEPIPES FOR IRRIGATION

If you have old leaky hosepipes, put them to good use. Simply make extra holes in the damaged one, block its end with a stopper and attach this pipe to the end of your new one. This makes a perfect watering mechanism to use in the vegetable garden. It does not cause splashes and gets the water right to the root area of the plants – a home-made form of drip irrigation.

DON'T FORGET THE RAINLESS AREAS

Remember to water the areas under the eaves of the house where the rain does not reach. It may pour with rain for days and yet some plants could be dying of thirst or lack of water.

WEEDS

REMOVE WEEDS AS SOON AS THEY APPEAR

Remember, the *first* golden rule for all weeds: when it first appears get it out, and then you won't have to apply the *second* golden rule: remove any flowers before they can set seed. This immediately reduces the risk of the weed spreading. Remember also that it is said that 'one year's seeding makes seven years' weeding!'

MAKE THAT WEEDKILLER STICK

Always choose weedkiller with a wetting agent as it increases its efficacy – a thin film of the chemical will stick to the entire surface of the leaf ensuring the maximum amount of weedkiller is absorbed.

BE RUTHLESS WITH PERENNIAL WEEDS

● Perennial weeds, such as stinging nettles, have underground stems and roots that act as storage compartments for the plant, ensuring it survives winter to emerge in spring. These need to be completely dug out, sometimes even with the soil around their roots, and thrown into the rubbish bin. (Don't put these on the compost heap, as they will simply grow again when the compost is returned to the garden.)

● A slower method of killing them is by the continuous removal of their leaves, which will weaken the plants slowly until they die. This is a long and tedious process and you have to be relentless about it.

● Another method is to use a systemic weedkiller to enter the leaf and travel down the plant, killing off the roots. These weeds will then need to be dug out by hand, together with their soil, and thrown away.

KEEP BARE GROUND
TO A MINIMUM

The only reason that weeds grow is because nothing else is growing in that particular spot or the soil is not covered by a mulch or hard landscaping such as brick paving material or gravel paths. The best form of weed prevention is to plant vigorous-growing groundcovers over the area, making it difficult for weeds to grow as they have to compete for light and water. In borders, plant your ornamental plants close together so there is little bare soil for weeds to grow – simply try to shade them out.

SPRAY ON SUNNY, WINDLESS, DRY DAYS

Always wait for a windless, hot day before you spray weedkillers. Even a slight wind could blow the poison onto other plants, with devastating effects. Similarly, never spray if there is a chance of rain on that day, as the rain will wash off the weedkiller, even if it contains a wetting agent. Ensure you target the exact plant you want killed and be sure that you cover the entire plant with the solution. Some weedkillers are available as gels which are simply painted onto the weed foliage with a brush. This ensures you kill the weeds and avoid contact with the surrounding plants.

HOE TO ELIMINATE WEEDS

Using a hoe is probably the most effective way of dealing with weeds and is the safest weedkiller for use around established plants. You can deal with many more plants at a time than by pulling them out by hand and it's safer to use than any poison. The only drawback is that it requires patience and exercise, and is only effective for use on annual weeds.

USE A SELECTIVE WEEDKILLER ON LAWNS

To avoid killing off your grass with the weeds, consult with someone at your local nursery as to which product would be best suited to your problem. Take a sample of the weed into the nursery for the best diagnosis.

Most manufacturers of weedkillers for use on lawns recommend that you first fertilize the lawn and the weeds, apply lots of water, and once the weeds and the grass are growing vigorously you apply the chemical. This ensures that the weeds are soft and juicy and will absorb the weedkiller more efficiently. However this also leads to the appearance of yellow patches in the grass as the lawn is also affected by the weedkiller, but fortunately the grass does recover with time. Don't be too concerned about these patches – continue to water and feed during this stressful period.

USE PLASTIC UNDER GRAVEL PATHS

When constructing pathways made of gravel or bark chips, put a plastic lining under the gravel to stop weeds growing through. Remember also to punch some holes in the plastic lining to allow water to seep through. The plastic lining will also prevent the gravel from mixing with the soil beneath it, and so will ensure that it stays clean and free of soil.

DO NOT DIG THE SOIL OVER TO WEED IT

Digging merely brings to the surface fresh weed seeds that were lying dormant under the soil surface. In the case of plants that form little bulbs, such as oxalis, you disturb the mother plant, causing the small bulblets to detach and start growing. In this case remove the plant and all the surrounding soil to the bin for removal. Never place these bulblets on the compost heap as they will end up back in the garden.

ZEN GARDENING

'LIFE BEGINS THE DAY YOU START A GARDEN.'
Chinese Proverb

INDEX

Page numbers in **bold** indicate headings.

First published in the UK in 2005 by
New Holland Publishers (UK) Ltd
London • Auckland • Sydney • Cape Town
www.newhollandpublishers.com

Garfield House, 86-88 Edgware Road, London W2 2EA
14 Aquatic Drive, Frenchs Forest NSW 2086 , Australia
218 Lake Road , Northcote , Auckland , New Zealand
80 McKenzie Street, Cape Town, 8001, South Africa

Printed by Times Offset, Malaysia

Publishing manager: Dominique le Roux
Managing editor: Lesley Hay-Whitton
Design director: Janice Evans
Designer: Alison Day
Consultant: Jo Smith
Cover photograph: www.jdlewis-photos.com

ISBN 1 84537 002 3

1 3 5 7 9 10 8 6 4 2